LIFE

THE AMERICAN SPIRIT

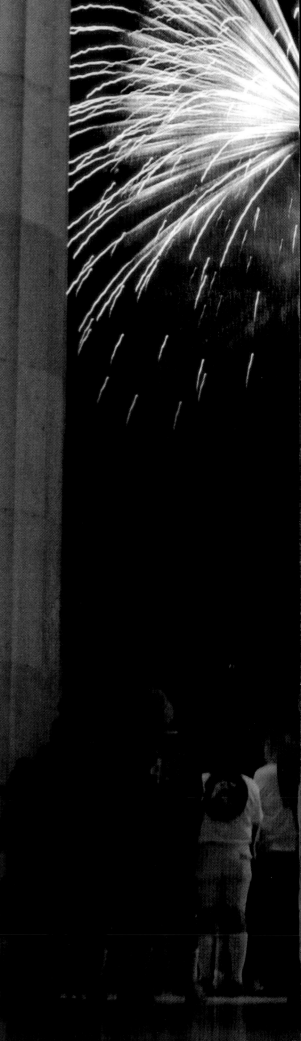

On these pages: the Fourth of July fireworks in Washington, D.C., as seen from the Lincoln Memorial. Photograph by David S. Holloway

The book's endpapers feature a double-exposure photograph by Gregg Brown that has a fascinating genesis. On a sunny morning in May 2001, Brown, while trying out a new camera lens, took two pictures of the lower Manhattan skyline. He rewound the film so he could use the remainder of the roll later, and tossed it into his camera bag. On September 15, Brown was asked by the Federal Emergency Management Agency to take aerial photographs of the destruction at Ground Zero (please see page 28). He hastily grabbed whatever film he could find. When he developed the pictures from that day's shoot, he was astonished to find this double exposure. "The photograph is an incredible coincidence," Brown says. "I believe it's an act of fate."

Apix

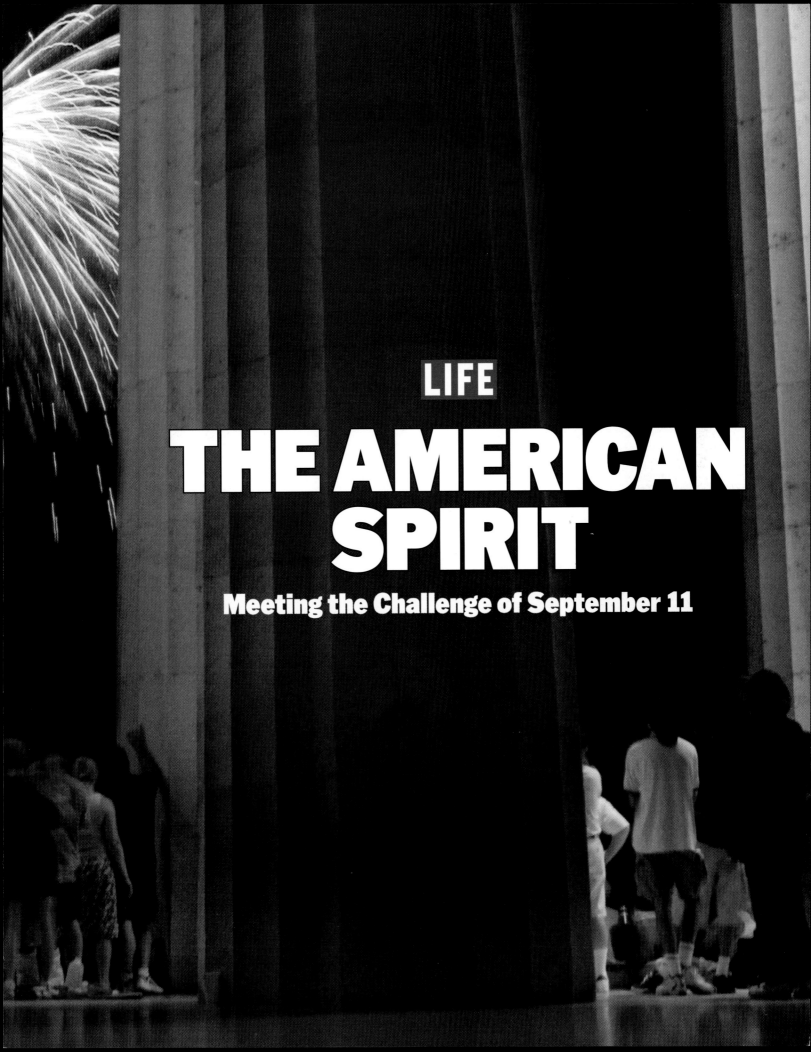

LIFE

THE AMERICAN SPIRIT

Meeting the Challenge of September 11

LIFE

Editor Robert Sullivan
Creative Director Ian Denning
Picture Editor Barbara Baker Burrows
Senior Editor Robert Andreas
Associate Picture Editor Christina Lieberman
Senior Reporter Hildegard Anderson
Writer/Reporters
Lauren Nathan, Rachel Silverman
Copy J.C. Choi (Chief), Stacy Sabraw
Production Manager Michael Roseman
Picture Research Lauren Steel
Photo Assistant Joshua Colow
Consulting Picture Editor (London)
Suzanne Hodgart

Publisher Andrew Blau
Director of Business Development Marta Bialek
Finance Director Camille Sanabria
Assistant Finance Manager Karen Tortora

Editorial Operations Richard K. Prue (Director),
Richard Shaffer (Manager), Brian Fellows, Raphael
Joa, Stanley E. Moyse (Supervisors), Keith Aurelio,
Gregg Baker, Charlotte Coco, Scott Dvorin, Kevin Hart,
Rosalie Khan, Sandra Maupin, Po Fung Ng,
Barry Pribula, David Spatz, Vaune Trachtman,
Sara Wasilausky, David Weiner

Time Inc. Home Entertainment

President Rob Gursha
Vice President, Branded Businesses David Arfine
Executive Director, Marketing Services
Carol Pittard
Director, Retail & Special Sales Tom Mifsud
Director of Finance Tricia Griffin
Marketing Director Kenneth Maehlum
Assistant Director Ann Marie Ross
Prepress Manager Emily Rabin
Associate Book Production Manager
Jonathan Polsky
Associate Product Manager Jennifer Dowell
Assistant Product Manager Michelle Kuhr

Special thanks to Suzanne DeBenedetto, Robert
Dente, Gina Di Meglio, Anne-Michelle Gallero,
Peter Harper, Natalie McCrea, Jessica McGrath,
Mary Jane Rigoroso, Steven Sandonato, Bozena
Szwagulinski, Niki Whelan

Published by

LIFE Books

Time Inc.
1271 Avenue of the
Americas, New York,
NY 10020

Library of Congress
Control Number:
2002106440
ISBN: 1-929049-88-0

"LIFE" is a trademark
of Time Inc.

We welcome your
comments and
suggestions about LIFE
Books. Please write to
us at: LIFE Books,
Attention: Book Editors,
PO Box 11016, Des
Moines, IA 50336-1016

If you would like to
order any of our
hardcover Collector's
Edition books, please
call us at 1-800-327-
6388. (Monday through
Friday, 7:00 a.m.–8:00
p.m. or Saturday, 7:00
a.m.–6:00 p.m. Central
Time).

Please visit us, and
sample past editions of
LIFE, at www.LIFE.com

At the Village Hall in Ridgefield, N.J., Edwin Winfield passes under Old Glory. PHOTOGRAPH BY STEVE SIMON

On May 30, 2002, onlookers line Building No. 3 of the World Financial Center, opposite Ground Zero in New York City, and bear witness to a ceremony marking the close of recovery efforts.

PHOTOGRAPH BY JAMES SALZANO

Introduction
by President George W. Bush

A year has passed since the day that forever changed our country. Debris from what once was the World Trade Center has been cleared away in a hundred thousand truckloads. The west side of the Pentagon looks almost as it did on September 10. And as families come home from summer vacations and children return to school, life seems almost normal.

Yet we are a different Nation today: sadder and stronger, less innocent and more courageous, more appreciative of life—and for many who serve our country, more willing to risk life in a great cause. For those who have lost family and friends, the pain will never go away—and neither will the responsibilities thrust upon us that day.

In a single instant, Americans realized that this will be a decisive decade in the history of liberty, that we have been called to a unique role in human events. Rarely has the world faced a choice more clear and consequential.

We face an enemy of ruthless ambition, unconstrained by law or morality. The terrorists despise other religions and have defiled their own. And they are determined to expand the scale and scope of their murder. The terror that targeted New York and Washington could next strike any center of civilization. Against such an enemy, there is no immunity, and there can be no neutrality.

Many nations and many families have lived in the shadow of terrorism for decades—enduring years of mindless, merciless killing. September 11 was not the beginning of global terror, but it was the beginning of the world's concerted response. History will remember that day not only as a day of tragedy but as a day of decision—when the civilized world was stirred to anger and to action. And the terrorists will remember September 11 as the day their reckoning began.

A mighty coalition of civilized nations is now defending our common security. More than 90 nations have arrested or detained more than 2,400 terrorists. All told, 130 nations are helping us track thousands of terrorist operatives through intelligence and law enforcement. Terrorist assets have been frozen. Terrorist front groups have been exposed. A terrorist regime has been toppled from power in Afghanistan. Our military is raiding al-Qaeda hiding places. We have captured and are interrogating terrorist leaders. From them, and from hundreds of other prisoners, we are learning more about how the terrorists operate, how they plan, and what their capabilities are. This information is crucial in anticipating and preventing future attacks.

Every day in this war will not bring the drama of liberating a country. Yet every day brings new information—a tip or arrest, another step or two or three in a relentless march to bring security to our Nation and justice to our enemies.

In defending the peace, we face a threat with no precedent. Enemies in the past needed great armies and great industrial capabilities to endanger our Nation. The attacks of September 11 required a few hundred thousand dollars in the hands of a few evil and deluded men. All the chaos and suffering they caused came at much less than the cost of a single tank.

The gravest threat to freedom today lies at the perilous crossroads of terror and technology. With the spread of chemical, biological and nuclear weapons, along with ballistic missile technology, even weak states and small groups could attain a catastrophic power to strike great nations. Our enemies have declared this very intention, and have been caught seeking these terrible weapons. They want the capability to blackmail us, or to harm us, or to harm our friends. We will oppose them with all our power.

For much of the last century, America's defense

The President, aboard the helicopter *Marine One* on September 14, 2001, views for the first time the dreadful ruin that is New York's Ground Zero.

tion treaties and then systematically break them. If we wait for threats to fully materialize, we will have waited too long.

Homeland defense and missile defense are part of stronger security, and they are essential priorities for America. Yet the war on terror will not be won on the defensive. We must take the battle to the enemy, disrupt his plans, and confront the worst threats before they emerge. In the world we have entered, the only path to safety is the path of action. And this Nation will act. We will lift this dark threat from our country and the world.

None of us would ever wish the evil that was done on September 11. Yet after America was attacked, it was as if our entire country looked into a mirror and saw our better selves. We were reminded that we are citizens, with obligations to each other, to our country, and to history. We began to think less about the goods we can accumulate, and more about the good we can do.

Many ask, "What can I do to help in our fight?" The answer is simple. All of us can become a September 11 volunteer by making a commitment to service in our own communities. You can serve your country by tutoring or mentoring a child, comforting the afflicted, housing those in need of shelter, building a new home. Whatever your talent, whatever your background, each of you can do something.

During my State of the Union Address last January, I asked all Americans to give at least two years, or 4,000 hours over their lives, to serving others. And I created the USA Freedom Corps to help Americans find volunteer opportunities.

America needs retired doctors and nurses who can be mobilized in emergencies, volunteers to help police and fire departments, and transportation and utility workers trained to spot danger. We have created a new Citizens Corps to enable Americans to make their own neighborhoods safer.

America needs citizens to strengthen our communities. We need more talented teachers in our troubled schools and more mentors to love our children. Through the USA Freedom Corps, we will expand and improve the good efforts of AmeriCorps and Senior Corps to meet the needs of America's communities. The USA Freedom Corps is also

rested on the cold war doctrines of deterrence and containment. In some cases, those strategies still apply. But new threats also require new thinking. Deterrence—the promise of massive retaliation against nations—means nothing against shadowy terrorist networks with no nation or citizens to defend. Containment is not possible when unbalanced dictators with weapons of mass destruction can deliver those weapons on missiles or secretly provide them to terrorist allies.

We cannot defend America and our friends by hoping for the best. We cannot put our faith in the word of tyrants, who solemnly sign nonprolifera-

working with the nonprofits, hospitals, houses of worship and schools around the country that offer millions of Americans the chance to serve.

And America needs citizens to extend the compassion of our country to every part of the world. So we are renewing the promise of the Peace Corps, doubling its volunteers over the next five years, and asking it to expand its efforts to foster education and development in the Islamic world. We will fight resentment and hatred with hope and progress.

As our Nation confronts new and unprecedented dangers, our citizens have new and important responsibilities. We must be vigilant. We will not give in to exaggerated fears or passing rumors. We will rely on good judgment and common sense. We will care for those who have lost loved ones, and comfort those who at times feel afraid.

We will not judge fellow Americans by appearance, ethnic background or religious faith. We will defend the values of our country, and we will live by them. We will persevere in this struggle, no matter how long it takes to prevail.

Above all, we will live in a spirit of courage and optimism. Our Nation was born in that spirit, as immigrants yearning for freedom courageously risked their lives in search of greater opportunity.

> **"America is embracing a new ethic and a new creed: 'Let's roll.'"**

That spirit of courage and optimism still beckons people across the world who want to come here. And that spirit of courage and optimism must guide those of us fortunate enough to live here.

On the morning of September 11, courage and optimism led the passengers on Flight 93 to rush their murderers to save lives on the ground. They were led by a young man whose last known words were the Lord's Prayer and "Let's roll." He did not know that he had signed on for heroism when he boarded the plane that day. Yet had he and his fellow passengers not acted, September 11's death toll could have been far higher.

For too long our culture has said, "If it feels good, do it." Now America is embracing a new ethic and a new creed: "Let's roll." In the sacrifice of soldiers, the fierce brotherhood of firefighters and the bravery and generosity of ordinary citizens, we have glimpsed what a new culture of responsibility could look like. We want to be a Nation that serves goals larger than self. We have been offered a unique opportunity, and we must not let this moment pass.

History has called our Nation into action. History has placed a great challenge before us: Will America—with our unique position and power—blink in the face of terror, or lead to a freer, more civilized world? There is only one answer: This great country will lead the world to safety, security, peace and freedom.

LONG MAY SHE WAVE

America has always been proud to say, "This is what we stand for."

In a groundswell of patriotism not seen since World War II, Americans turned to Old Glory to show their feelings, as seen here, on May 22, in Windsor, N.C.

Flags and banners are used today for everything from display to decoration, from signaling to selling. But in their traditional and most important roles, they serve as a means of indicating an allegiance, and as a rallying point for like-feeling people. Flags unify a citizenry and speak, symbolically, of societal beliefs and values. To attack a flag is to attack its country—and vice versa. Today, as in ancient Asia, where flags first unfurled 3,000 years ago, the fall of the colors means defeat.

Whether or not the design that was ratified by an Act of the American Congress on June 14, 1777, was first rendered in bulldog cotton by George Washington's friend, the Philadelphia seamstress Betsy Ross, is inconsequential here.

Of undoubted relevance, though, in light of the attacks of September 11, is what the American flag has stood for from the very beginning. As a whole, it registered the proud defiance of a colonial people in the face of tyrannical rule by Great Britain.

Betsy Ross and two of her "children"—the flag below waved for Francis Scott Key; at right, New York, 1941.

In its parts, the flag bore other messages. The 13 stripes represented the coming together of a baker's dozen colonies. So did, according to the Congressional resolution, the "thirteen stars, white in a blue field, representing a new constellation."

Red, white and blue. The colors were not casually chosen, and if one elects to read more into it, September 11, as with the new constellation of stars, can be viewed cosmically. The white, symbolizing Purity and Innocence, was assaulted on that day. The red, standing for Hardiness and Valor, responded to the violence. The blue, representing Vigilance, Perseverance and Justice, remains dedicated to the creation of a more stable world.

Before nightfall on that fateful day, it was manifestly clear that the foes of the United States had not brought down the flag. Rather, they had caused it to bloom across the land—indeed, around the world. It flew at half-staff and full; it fluttered from truck antennas and from countless rooftops. A flag that had been claimed from a yacht in New York Harbor by a group of firefighters, then raised high above the rubble of Ground Zero, became arguably as famous as those star-spangled banners that flew at Fort McHenry and atop Iwo Jima's Mount Suribachi. The Ground Zero flag eventually traveled the country, frail and beleaguered, appearing at somber commemorations and at all-American extravaganzas like the Super Bowl. It was saluted and cheered.

Some speculated that all these flags would tatter and finally vanish as September 11 receded from view. That hasn't happened. Faded and worn flags have been replaced, as the American spirit, unquestionably bruised and frayed itself, has found resilience and a new sense of purpose in judging itself against the spirit of the enemy. America and its allies have raised Old Glory, declaring, "Here's what we stand for." These many months later, they have yet to see the enemy's flag.

Dennis Brack/Black Star

At left, two members of American Legion Post 364, Billy Moriarity (foreground) and Kevin Morley, hang flags from the Prince William Parkway bridge over I-95 in Woodbridge, Va., on September 14. That same day, not far from the Pentagon, the man below departs a prayer service in Arlington, Va.

David S. Holloway/Apix

Flags large and small carry the message. Above, not long after the attacks, the DeCarlos of Lexington, Mass., painted the Stars and Stripes on their house. Below, New York's Finest march in the 75th annual Macy's Thanksgiving Day Parade in 2001. At left, nine-year-old Californian Amble Neukum delights to the Salt Lake City Olympic Games in February 2002.

The Passage of the Seasons

As time went on, even humor was allowed to return, along with criticism and second-guessing. But a deep sense of purpose prevailed. So, too, a nagging anxiety. September 11 continued to inform everything about life in America.

President George W. Bush at a Sarasota, Fla., school on September 11, before the towers fell

Eric Draper/The White House

> **Today we say to those who masterminded this cruel plot, and to those who carried it out, that the spirit of this nation will not be defeated by their twisted and diabolical schemes.**
>
> — the Reverend Billy Graham

> **I want justice. And there's an old poster out west, that I recall, that said, 'Wanted, Dead or Alive.'**
>
> — President George W. Bush

> **It's six degrees of separation. It will be very personal.**
>
> — Bessel van der Kolk, Boston University professor of psychiatry, on how the aftershocks of the attacks will spread throughout the country

> **When you go to work, you be the tower. You stand tall.**
>
> — the Reverend Calvin Butts, to workers in New York City's financial district

> **Who the hell in the FBI has ever seen weapons-grade anthrax powder? They, as well as the doctors at the CDC, know nothing about the behavior of the spore in aerosol, and this is the secret to the whole shooting match. I can see where the public would be thoroughly confused.**
>
> — William Patrick III, veteran biological weapons designer, on ignorance concerning anthrax

> **I think it's prudent to prepare for a mass-casualty event.**
>
> — Raymond Zilinskas, former U.N. bioweapons inspector, on anthrax

Mark Peterson/Corbis Saba

> **It's time to get back to life.**
>
> — Lisa Beamer, as she boarded the same flight her late husband, Todd, had taken on September 11

> **I even have single moms coming in and telling me they want to have another child so that should something happen to them, their first child won't be left alone.**
>
> — Dr. Iffath Hoskins, New York City obstetrician, on childbearing in the wake of September 11

> **Afghans are used to hard tasks. They will never lose their jihad morale.**
>
> — Mullah Mohammed Omar, leader of the Taliban

> **We have no more to do with Osama bin Laden than you do. He certainly doesn't represent Islam, and we're just devastated.**
>
> — Sheryl Siddiqui, member of the board of the Islamic Society of Tulsa

> **I think this whole thing has been especially difficult for young people, because our generation has been defined by O.J., Monica Lewinsky, stuff that was really trivia. Our generation has never had anything real to deal with.**
>
> — Andrew Karpinski, age 23, who decided after September 11 to join AmeriCorps, a program that sends volunteers to work in struggling communities

> **It was almost therapeutic. It doesn't change the tragedy. But life does go on, at some point. It does.**
>
> — Scott Brosius, New York Yankees third baseman, on returning to baseball after September 11

> **I encourage Americans to assemble in their homes, places of worship or community centers to reinforce ties of family and community, express our profound thanks for the many blessings we enjoy, and reach out in true gratitude and friendship to our friends around the world.**
>
> — President Bush, in his Thanksgiving proclamation

Chris Usher/Corbis Sygma

❝ There's not much the average New Yorker can do to help anymore. Everything seems to be taken. Things are getting back to normal in New York. The other day a driver yelled, 'Get a life,' and gave me the finger. ❞

— Ground Zero volunteer

Christopher Morris/VII

❝ We don't know where bin Laden is. We've been pretty honest about that. We've said he is either dead or alive, and he is either inside Afghanistan or he isn't. ❞

— Army Gen. Tommy Franks, chief of the U.S. Central Command

❝ One of the greatest spiritual revivals in the history of America. People are turning to God. The churches are full. ❞

— Pat Robertson, Christian broadcaster, on a religious renaissance in the wake of September 11

❝ I just don't see much indication that there has been a great awakening or a profound change in America's religious practices. It looks like people were treating this like a bereavement, a shorter-term funeral kind of thing, where they went to church or synagogue to grieve. But once past that, their normal churchgoing behavior passed back to where it was. ❞

— Frank M. Newport, editor in chief of the Gallup Poll

❝ Evil knows no holiday. ❞

— President Bush, announcing cancellation of the White House Christmas tours

Andrew Savulich/Daily News

❝ In a disaster situation, the Red Cross offers aid to people regardless of income. It's up to you whether you want to accept it. ❞

— Edward Hardy, Red Cross spokesman, on why donations were extended to all, needy or not, living below Canal Street in Manhattan

❝ This is not an argument about whether to get rid of Saddam Hussein. That debate is over. This is . . . how you do it. ❞

— Senior administration official

AP/Department of Defense

❝ They were overjoyed when the first plane hit the building, so I said to them, 'Be patient.' ❞

— Osama bin Laden, on a videotape, telling of his al-Qaeda associates' reaction to the attacks

❝ We're chasing a person who encourages young people to go kill themselves, and he, himself, refuses to stand and fight. ❞

— President Bush, on the hunt for Osama bin Laden

New York Stock Exchange Christmas tree, Broad Street

Gamma

" We're survivors, you and I. We will be defined not by the lives we led until the 11th of September, but by the lives we will lead from now on. "

— Bill Moyers, journalist

" Hi! It looks pretty dicey from here—at least your papers don't run front-page photos of the corpses of journalists. "

— Daniel Pearl, *Wall Street Journal* reporter, in an E-mail to his mother, Judea, two months before his abduction

Elise Amendola/AP

" The flight attendant . . . appeared to have prevented something very serious from occurring. "

— Thomas Kinton, Massachusetts Port Authority, on the subduing of shoe-bomb suspect Richard Reid (left)

" People want to say there isn't racial profiling at the airport, but let's be honest. If your first name is Muhammad, and your last name isn't Ali, leave a little extra time. "

— Jay Leno

" Danny was an outstanding colleague, a great reporter, and a dear friend of many at the *Journal*. His murder is an act of barbarism that makes a mockery of everything Danny's kidnappers claimed to believe in. "

— Paul Steiger, managing editor of *The Wall Street Journal*

" A lot of people expect they should be over this by now. They say 'I should have forgotten this by now, it didn't happen to me . . . ' But this is something in the consciousness that was never there before. It's an imprint; it's like something that gets etched into us. And some people are in a kind of meltdown. "

— Dr. Laurie Nadel, psychologist

" I think people will move less in the coming year. I think people will feel a sense that sameness is related to security, and I think people will want to be close to their families. "

— Jerome Rosenberg, associate professor of psychology, University of Alabama, Tuscaloosa

" Imagining evil of this magnitude simply does not come naturally to the American character, which is why, even after we are repeatedly confronted with it, we keep reverting to our natural, naively optimistic selves. "

— Thomas L. Friedman, *New York Times* columnist

" The prospect of another attack against the U.S. is very, very real . . . Not a matter of if, but when. "

— Vice President Dick Cheney

" It's going to be worse, and a lot of people are going to die. I don't think there's a damn thing we're going to be able to do about it. "

— Anonymous U.S. counterterrorism official, on future terrorist attacks

" I have made mistakes occasionally in my public comments based on information or a lack of information that I subsequently got. "

— FBI Director Robert S. Mueller III, on whether the Bureau had missed warning signs of the terrorist attacks

Lloyd Francis Jr./Sipa

" I think the people in Washington should not be focusing on who knew what, when or where. I think they should be focusing on what's coming. "

— Patrick Cartier Sr., whose son died in the World Trade Center

" They have chemical weapons . . . biological weapons . . . some shortly will have nuclear weapons. "

— Secretary of Defense Donald Rumsfeld

" I hope that as we families sit together and listen to the tape we will, amid all the violence and confusion and ugliness, be able to recognize some brief familiar voices of our heroic sons and daughters, husbands and wives. "

— Alice Hoglan, a United flight attendant, before listening to the tape of the Flight 93 hijacking. Her son had been a passenger on the plane, and she believes he helped try to rush the cockpit.

Mark Wilson/Getty

Spencer Platt/Getty

Vietnam War veteran Stephen Smallwood, 135th Kings County Memorial Day Parade, Brooklyn, NY

❝ **The difference is night and day. We were attacked, and while I never paid much attention to the military, today I welcome this parade.** ❞

— an anonymous former Vietnam War protestor who had never before attended a Memorial Day parade

❝ **We need to accept that the possibility of terrorism is a permanent condition for the foreseeable future. We just have to accept it.** ❞

— Tom Ridge, Director of Homeland Security

PF Bentley

> **To break the unbending will of the American people is impossible.**
>
> — Alik Sarkisian, a regional chief in Ararat, Armenia, at the unveiling of an obelisk commemorating the victims of September 11

Laura Rauch/AP

Fireworks, Fourth of July, Washington, D.C.

Stefan Zaklin/Apix

> **This is a terrorist attack. But it won't stop us from making this country a safer place.**
>
> — An Afghan foreign ministry spokesman on the assassination of Vice President Hajji Abdul Qadir (above)

> **Our martyrs are ready for operations against American and Jewish targets inside and outside. America should be prepared. It should be ready. They should fasten the seatbelts. We are coming to them where they never expected.**
>
> — Sulaiman Abu Ghaith, al-Qaeda spokesman

> **It's like ice cream for my eyes.**
>
> — Three-year-old Joshua Roseman, watching Fourth of July fireworks in Margaretville, N.Y.

> **Bush is competing with Sharon to be the most hated leader among Palestinians.**
>
> — Ahmed Tibi, Israeli Arab Knesset member

> **The best way to be safe is for all of us to move into the middle of the desert and live in some subterranean cavern, but we can't do that.**

— Washington, D.C., Mayor Anthony Williams

Broward County (Fla.) Sheriff's Office/AP

> **He was trying to build something that would attain a nuclear yield.**

— A senior Bush administration official on alleged "dirty bomber" Jose Padilla

> **These are shadowy killers, and we're treating them just as they are—as international crooks, international criminals . . . these are the kind of folks that will slip into a city and try to hide, or they'll go to a cave and then they'll send some youngster to his death.**

— President Bush, in a speech thanking Homeland Security workers

> **Just about anybody who's dysfunctional to start with can get wrapped up in this Islamic-extremist world.**

— A senior U.S. intelligence official

> **It's like the networks are a how-to manual for terrorists. You see them on the news. This reporter is standing outside a water-treatment plant, going, 'If they poured the poison here it could wipe out thousands because the guard is off duty from noon until one every day!'**

— Jay Leno

> **This snake can crawl without its head.**

— Dick Armey, House Majority Leader, emphasizing that al-Qaeda can function without Osama bin Laden

> **We are not going to see fundamental, solid change in airport security for several years hence yet. There's an awful lot of promise but not an awful lot of substance at this moment in time.**

— Chris Yates, airport security analyst

Reuters

> **In the supermarket, all you hear people talking about is what's made in America, and not to buy it.**

— Saudi housewife

> **So he hear every day, somebody killed by Israelis, somebody got shot by Israelis. He got angry. He got angry, so he explode.**

— A former employee of Hisham Mohammed Hedayet, who was killed after opening fire at an El Al ticket counter at LAX

Paul Parkus/Los Angeles Times

Meredith McKeown

Gregg Brown's Photographic Odyssey

He was, on September 11, a 30-year-old lifelong New Yorker with an apartment on the Lower East Side. It was only on the 14th that he found himself ready to go out again. "The city was still chaotic," he recalls. "I walked up First Avenue with my girlfriend Janna. At Bellevue Hospital there was a wall with victims' pictures. We paid tribute, and I said, 'I wish there was a way I could help.'"

Brown wasn't obviously placed to do that. He wasn't a doctor; he wasn't a cop. He had his own small photography business in a city full of people with photography businesses. The ad in the Yellow Pages, designed to compete, said WE DO IT ALL and 24-HR RUSH JOBS WELCOME. "I mentioned everything but weddings," Brown says. "I made a decision to avoid weddings."

Gregg and Janna went to dinner at a nearly empty restaurant on the 14th, then headed back to the apartment. Meantime, Kathryn Humphrey at the Federal Emergency Management Agency was in consultation with the New York City fire and police departments about a plan to photograph Ground Zero from the air. Wouldn't it help us, they wondered, to know where these fires are going? To see if buildings are shifting?

FEMA officials flipped through the phone book and found a guy with 24-hour service. It was two a.m. when the phone rang.

"Do you do aerial photography?" was the question.

"Yes," Brown said. He had never taken a picture from the air.

From that morning until the shutdown of Ground Zero as a recovery site in late May 2002, Brown flew almost daily over the area, recording a remarkable story of devastation—and rebirth.

Lower Manhattan, facing southeast
May 7, 2002

RECLAIMING

GROUND ZERO

"I grabbed any film I could that first day. I found myself filled with adrenaline—and fear. For one thing, I had never been in a helicopter. The day began when a Sheriff's Department escort picked me up and took me through all the security to the copter. Before I got in, the pilot asked me, 'Have you seen it?' I said no. He said, 'It's unbelievable.' And, of course, it was."

The Twin Towers, facing east
September 15, 2001

"The 15th was really the first day that the smoke had cleared enough for a photographer to be able to see anything from the air. When I peered down, I was thinking about the news that was saying this was still a rescue operation— everyone remaining hopeful we'd find people alive. I remember thinking right away that there were no survivors in there.

Ground Zero, facing north

The World Trade Center, facing north, before September 11, 200:

Search and Rescue

At the outset, the operation was officially a rescue mission, and very little demolition or recovery work was done. The sad fact is, however, that the immensity of the devastation (more than 1.5 million tons of material came from the Twin Towers alone) and the intensity of the fires (perhaps 2000°F) were efficient in their killing. Including the passengers, crew and hijackers aboard the two planes, 2,825 people perished at New York's Ground Zero, and none were found alive after September 12. The building at the bottom of Brown's photo above and the satellite image at right is the Bankers Trust. At the top of Brown's photo are remnants of World Trade Center Buildings 5 and 6.

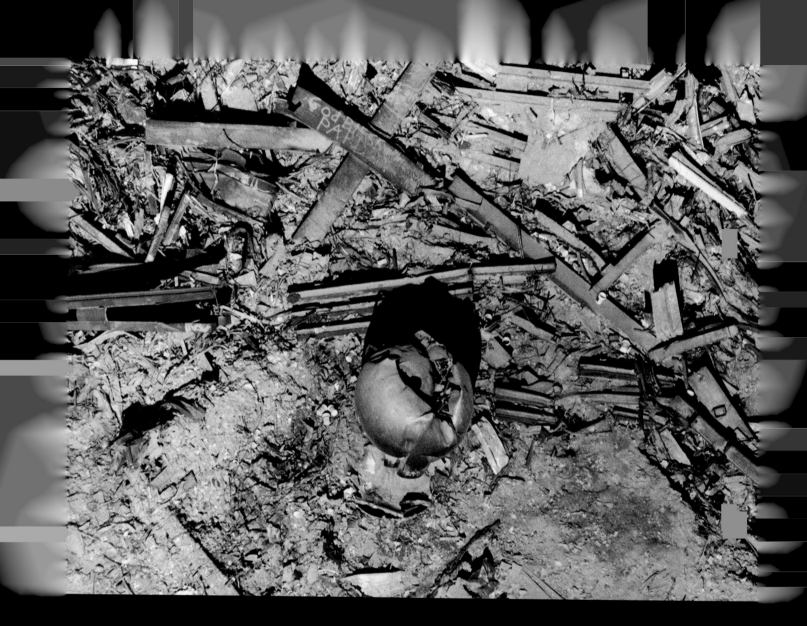

> **My job description was to photograph the site, but when I saw something of human significance, I tried to come in close on it. I thought it important to get the Sphere. When I saw the print, I noticed the Port Authority Police Department cross right next to it—that was remarkable. Months later it was uplifting to see the Sphere as a monument again in Battery Park.**

The Sphere Memorial, Battery Park, April 23, 2002

Ground Zero, facing north

Church Street, facing north, October 28, 2001

Early Memorials

The Sphere was a 15-foot-in-diameter, 45,000-pound bronze-and-steel sculpture by the German artist Fritz Koenig. A centerpiece of the World Trade Center plaza, it was meant to symbolize world peace through international trade. It was gashed and dented on September 11, but found structurally intact (indicated above). On March 11 it was reborn near the Hope Garden in Battery Park as the Sphere Memorial (opposite, bottom). At the dedication, Mayor Michael R. Bloomberg called the Sphere "a stirring tribute to the courage of those we lost and a reminder of the resiliency of the American Spirit." A Ground Zero memorial for those lost was held in late October (right).

Ground Zero, facing north

4 World Trade Center, facing southwest, November 10, 2001

The Recovery Speeds Up

Once the operation on the ground had evolved from rescue to recovery, says Brown, "work progressed very fast and the site started changing very quickly. Every day there was a massive amount accomplished." A first order of business was the demolition of ruined buildings. Cranes and hoses attended the taking down of Building No. 4 (above and right), one of the earliest removals. Building No. 6 would be the last to come down, and so its awesome crater of destruction loomed for weeks at the northwest corner of Ground Zero. "Obviously, the site was emotionally overwhelming," says Brown. "When working, I shut down that side of myself so I could do the job properly."

> *What I saw during the day would hit me more forcefully at night. I would close my eyes and I would see the site. I would see the steel of the towers. These buildings were just about exactly as old as I was, and had always been a part of the New York City I knew. I realized, in December, that I was recording their very last moments. Thoughts like that affected me very deeply during the project, and I found myself on an emotional roller coaster.*

The north tower, facing north
December 15, 2001

Ground Zero, facing north

6 World Trade Center, facing north, Christmas Eve, 2001

Last Vestiges of the Towers

They had once stood 110 floors each and, between them, contained some 10 million square feet of space. They were proud and gleaming symbols rising from the southern tip of Manhattan. But from September 11 into December, they were reduced to a far different—though no less iconic—imagery. The lattice-like remnants of the north tower's lowest floors became famous in photographs, as well as the principal focus of pilgrims to Ground Zero. But those symbols, too, had to come down, as did, finally, WTC Building No. 6 (right). By Christmas, Ground Zero had been brought to ground level. It was clear that the intensity of the effort had the project racing ahead of schedule.

February 22, 2002

May 31, 2002

Ground Zero, facing north

The Winter Garden, facing west, February 12, 2002

A Jewel Survives

Looking onto the Hudson to the west, but hidden by the mammoth Trade Center on its eastern side, was the World Financial Center's magnificent atrium, the Winter Garden (pointed out, above). Its 45,000 square feet of space, covered with 60,000 square feet of glass, provided a grand entrance to the city for the tens of thousands who would march through a grove of palm trees each morning. It was damaged in the attacks but not irretrievably. Currently undergoing a $50 million renovation with a self-imposed deadline of September 11, 2002, the Winter Garden will have a newly designed glass facade facing West Street, through which New Yorkers will watch the rebuilding of Ground Zero

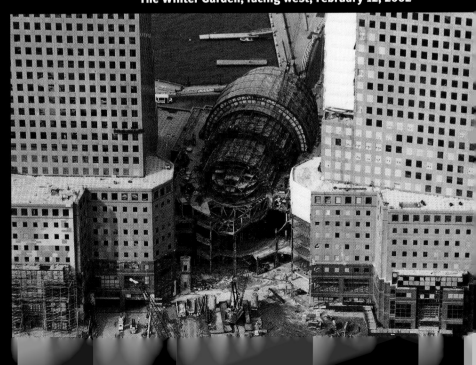

West Street, facing wes
March 19, 200

Ground Zero, facing north

The south tower site, facing southeast, March 12, 200

Rolling Again

Work continued at the astonishing pace, and by late winter the endgame for a project that was supposed to take much longer was very evidently approaching. Certainly the progress was being fueled by passion, as workers—more than 1,500 in all—put in 18-hour shifts, extra shifts, seven-day weeks, literally millions of man-hours. West Street (indicated above and seen in the photographs opposite) had been unearthed and was back in service by early spring. With the advent of warm weather, everything sped up still further. Almost every day, work would be halted as a discovery was being made. "You'd see them gather," Brown says, "You'd know they found a body."

> I won't be flying tomorrow, and I'll miss it. I'll miss watching the helicopter land and hearing over the radio, 'PD4 to pickup Downtown Gregg Brown'— always thinking, even after all these months, 'I can't believe they're here for me.' I'll miss the roar of the engine, the chatter of police radio. What I won't miss is the horror.

PATH World Trade Center
Terminal, facing northeast
May 8, 2002

Ground Zero, facing north

Liberty Street, facing south

A Ground Reclaimed

Months ahead of schedule, the recovery was officially declared complete on May 30. "The Bath-
tub" (above), whose western wall holds back the
Hudson (much of the site is built on landfill), was
clearly delineated. The cost of the cleanup came
to $750 million. More than 10,000 firefighters had
worked the site; more than 17 million meals had
been served; more than 100,000 volunteers had
put in time in and around Ground Zero; more than
a thousand victims had been identified; more than
1,600 death certificates issued. A proper sign was
draped at the south end of the site (right)—on the
properly named Liberty Street—and proper memorials were held. Then building began.

WE WILL NEVER FORGET

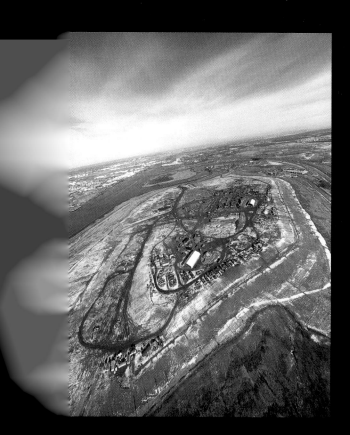

ACROSS THE HARBOR

A landfill had been closed only recently on Staten Island, which is a place unto itself but also one of New York City's five boroughs. The landfill was called Fresh Kills ("kill" is from the Dutch for "channel" or "creek"), and that is where the material from Ground Zero was brought. Officials say that 1,645,274 tons of debris—nearly twice the weight of the Golden Gate Bridge—were removed in 108,535 truckloads. And Fresh Kills can be seen statistically or coldly: In the photograph above, Manhattan is distant on the horizon; in the one at right, a hundred piles testify to daily deliveries. But it should be remembered that these pictures represent murder. "I started photographing Fresh Kills on September 24," says Brown. "That was a hard day. Ground Zero was where heroes had performed. This was, simply, a burial ground."

Toward an End

Two hundred FDNY vehicles reached Ground Zero on September 11, and 92 of them were lost. Scores of other cars and trucks were crushed. "But from the air you didn't think about numbers or equipment," says Brown. "You thought about the people. I saw men in their Haz Mat suits at Fresh Kills and knew what they were searching for. I hoped they would find it— some sign, some evidence that would bring closure for one more family. For some, I knew, there would never be an ending."

PILGRIMS

They make their way to Ground Zero
to witness, to mourn, to contemplate,
to pray. Photography by Steve Simon

SANCTUARY

At Ground Zero, a church survives, and finds its mission.
Photography by David Turnley

Another in a litany of closing ceremonies at Ground Zero, this one equally solemn, certainly as spiritual as the others. Those others, marking the end of the recovery phase and attended by survivors, families of victims, and dignitaries, are seen on the evening news and above the fold in newspapers coast to coast. This gathering, in a place untouched by September 11 except in a thousand affecting ways, is smaller and more intimate. As men and women—police, firefighters, construction workers, passersby—enter, they flash no passes, encounter no metal detectors. They don't quite fill the pews of St. Paul's Chapel this midday—Wednesday, May 29, 2002—for a "public service of thanksgiving" to commemorate the end of missionary service there. But they fill the small old church to overflowing with emotion heartfelt and profound.

Thanksgiving? At Ground Zero? Indeed. Thanksgiving that this church, which somehow has always been protected from tides of calamity, had again been spared. That in finding itself whole, it had found its mission, transforming itself from an underused Episcopalian house of God to a bustling, ecumenical hospice of relief, solace, rest and sanctuary. A place where all who visited or volunteered were, in the words of the pastor, "bathed in love."

In the days after the attacks, St. Paul's was called "the little church that stood," and while that's true—it does seem miraculous that this small building, so proximate to such devastation, went unscathed—it speaks only to the chapel's blessed survival, not to how the chapel realized its true calling. Over eight and a half months leading up to this day, St. Paul's established itself as the little church that did.

The stone church was built in 1766 and provided spiritual nourishment for George Washington. After September 11 it offered the same to retired firefighter John Misha and thousands of others.

Reverend Harris holds the chalice during the final Eucharist. Attendees include volunteers, people off the street and, in absentia, hundreds of kids who have sent expressions of goodwill.

What did it do? Whatever was required. Beginning on the 11th of September, it determined to practice what the Reverend Lyndon Harris is calling, from the pulpit, "the art of radical hospitality." Every establishment in the neighborhood that had not been destroyed was instantly altered on the 11th: Burger King became a police headquarters; Brooks Brothers became a morgue. St. Paul's became a drop-in center where rescue workers could find a moment's peace. Then, quite quickly, it grew into a well-organized hub where, for months, recovery workers could count on a meal, water, new boots and gloves, a rest or a rubdown, some spiritual or mental counseling, a daily Eucharist, an evening serenade, a bed. The public, beyond the 5,000 who volunteered to offer their radical hospitality, was kept out. The chapel belonged to the workers and searchers of Ground Zero; it was their space for healing and grieving.

"The poet said, 'mid-winter spring is its own season,'" says Reverend Harris in his homily. "The period spanning from the terrorist attacks until today is its own season," a time of "bringing order out of chaos." He calls it "a season of renewal" in which we have tried to reclaim "our humanity. Ultimately, what began in hatred has evolved," he claims, into "a season of love."

He can testify in this optimistic way because he has been at St. Paul's, has watched "lawyers, judges,

soccer moms and entrepreneurs . . . people who have risen to the scriptural challenge . . . 'to try and outdo one another in showing love.'" Back in the autumn of 2001, word about what was going on at St. Paul's started moving uptown and out to the suburbs, and suddenly an army of enlistees were asking how they could help. Music students from Juilliard went downtown to play harps and cellos. Caterers donated and served food. Chiropractors established a clinic in one corner of the church. Adjacent to George Washington's box, where the first President prayed for the success of his foundling nation, a community of cots was set up. Mark Maginn, secretary for the New York State Society for Clinical Social Work, lives in Irvington, just up the Hudson River. He heard about the work at St. Paul's "through the Episcopal grapevine." Soon he was one of those organizing mental-health volunteers to help Ground Zero workers through their ordeal. At any time of the day or night, soft-voiced

conversations were ongoing in the pews or up in the balcony, mingling with whispered prayers.

Maginn and many of his fellow volunteers are here today to give thanks and say farewell, as are many of those they served. John Misha is here. A large, strong, retired firefighter from New Jersey, he has spent so much time at St. Paul's over eight and a half months, he considers the church his second home. Misha of Engine 69, a 20-year veteran of the FDNY, worked nearly a hundred 12-to-15-hour tours of duty at Ground Zero, much more than the average firefighter. When his clothes were wet, he exchanged them at St. Paul's for dry ones; when it was cold, he found extra layers to wear; one day, a podiatrist removed a painful callus from his foot. "All day I worked with death," he says. "At St. Paul's I found life." But next week it will be closed, and all searching ended. What will he do? "I don't know," he says, tears welling.

The Episcopal grapevine extends beyond Irv-

Before the service, a police officer and a firefighter slump in the pews as they reflect on the tragedy that occurred nearby and—perhaps—on the grace within these walls. During the service, sanitation engineers, police, construction workers, ironworkers and firefighters are represented at the chapel's podium.

ington, and churches nationwide learned of St. Paul's good works. Food, supplies and letters started arriving. School kids individually or through class projects sent messages of support, and these were taped everywhere in the church. "Here's my angel," wrote a boy named Blake, who had drawn a cheerful, orange-haired spirit. "It's quite small as you can tell. It will guard you until all is well." Another child copied words from 1 John 4:16: "And so we know and rely on the love God has for us. God is love. Whoever lives in love lives in God and God in him." The fourth- and fifth-graders from Cedar Springs, Mich., made a huge flag using the shapes of their many hands, and it is broadly displayed from the balcony. Meanwhile, a note from Allison of Edgecome, Maine, affixed to the back of a pew, quietly expresses the hope that "if all of us work together then we can save America."

Those children aren't here today, but many people are who were buoyed by their words. Some of

Social worker Maginn harmonizes on a hymn with his fellow volunteer Andrea Ralya, who oversaw all the mission's operations at least two nights each and every week.

them speak during the service. Construction worker Tom Geraghty says he watched the towers fall from a spot on Greenwich Street, knowing well that his beloved sister-in-law was inside. "For months, I cursed God, hated him, until I came to this chapel—this sanctuary, this refuge from the devastation, this kitchen, this bathroom, this doctor's office, this bedroom, this therapist's couch, this music hall, this massage table, this little cafe on Broadway. This

place helped me and so many others to heal slowly each day, to get my thoughts and emotions back on track." In the end, he regained faith in God, faith tempered by a conviction: "He sure as hell must work in mysterious ways."

If Geraghty were the only person—not one of thousands—who had been helped by the mission, we would still say that the little church contributed mightily in the months after September 11. And if

St. Paul's helped people such as Geraghty, they helped St. Paul's in turn. The attacks not only spared St. Paul's, they also raised it up.

As mentioned earlier, St. Paul's had been left untouched by a maelstrom once before. In 1776 a great fire swept lower Manhattan, claiming acres of buildings, including the mother church to the south, Trinity. St. Paul's was, at that time, the newer and grander of the two—the one more needed by its congregation—and so a quickly organized bucket brigade extending from the Hudson River focused its effort on saving St. Paul's. When the smoke cleared, all around the chapel lay in ashes, but the church stood, and continued to fulfill the spiritual needs of its flock during a time of tragedy.

Through the dust-caked windows of St. Paul's on September 11, 2001, could be seen the devastation of the modern inferno. This time the church

Geraghty, in orange vest, prays to a God he not long ago cursed. After the Eucharist, hugs are general throughout St. Paul's, as no one chooses to exit the church quickly.

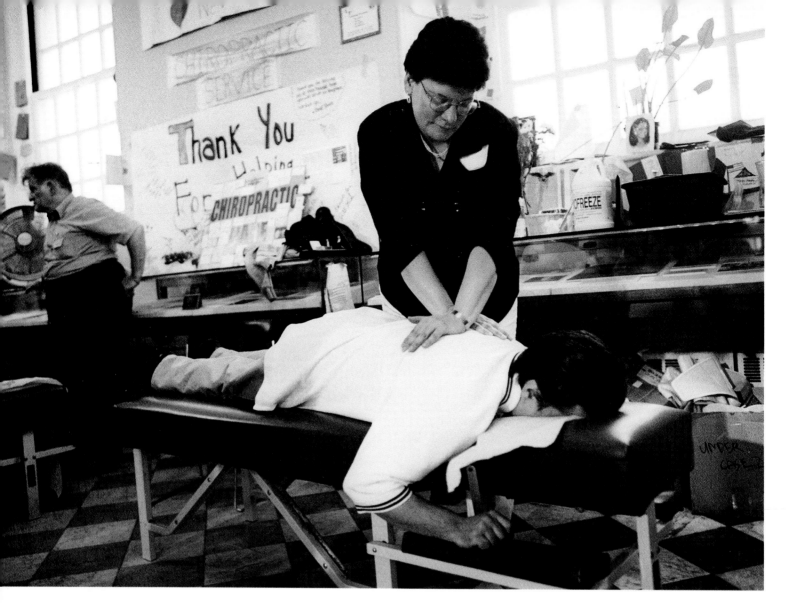

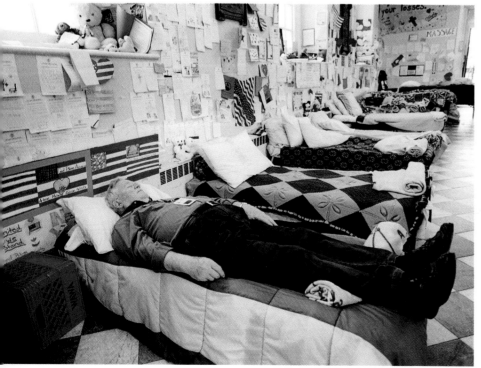

was not new but, rather, the oldest house of worship in the city. It had, truth be told, been all but forgotten in the skyscraper canyons of downtown. Few attended services there regularly, and if something regal or elegant was planned for a chapel in the Wall Street area, it was invariably scheduled for Trinity. Although little St. Paul's ran a men's shelter prior to September 11, its ministry was certainly not a hive of activity.

And then, it was spared yet again, just as in 1776. For what reason? St. Paul's didn't pause to ask the question. Its way was clear.

Those who attacked America on September 11 said it was about religion. That is clearly a subtext on this day, May 29, 2002. A congregation of dozens of different faiths is gathered here, declaring as one: All right then, this is about religion. What religion says is, Bathe one another in love. That's the way religion speaks to us. It speaks through young Blake's protecting angel, the quotation from John,

400,000 meals, the peaceful ecumenism of New York City, Tom Geraghty's bruised but intact faith. Says John Misha, the firefighter: "At St. Paul's, God was here with His arm around my shoulders."

The service nears its end. Blessing is bestowed, a hymn sung—"Come, Labor On"—and then the service arrives at what is simply called Dismissal. The admonition is "Go in peace." Now the ministers walk down the aisle to the rear of the church, their footfalls accompanied by a few sobs and final whispered prayers. The ministers mingle. The worshipers shift in the pews but stay there. Hugs are exchanged; strangers embrace; cops hug strangers; firefighters hug cops. There is no movement toward the doors. There is, instead, a palpable reluctance to have this thanksgiving service end. There is no will among these people to leave St. Paul's.

One small woman of a certain age, still seated and not at all inclined to budge, suggests an answer. "They feel safe in here," she says.

Tomorrow, May 30, the chapel will close for a cleaning, then reopen as a church. Today, its final day as Ground Zero's mission, the work that has gone on for months at St. Paul's continues. Massages are given, rest taken, music played. And, just as important, Blake's happy angel stands watch.

It Happened Once Before

The lower tip of Manhattan Island was host to Armageddon long before September 11, writes Daniel S. Levy. There was then, as now, a resolve to rise—quickly—from the ashes.

T he streets of lower Manhattan were "an ocean of fire," recalled Gabriel Disosway, who worked on Pearl Street, "with roaring, rolling, burning waves, surging onward and upward, and spreading certain universal destruction; tottering walls and falling chimneys, with black smoke, hissing, clashing sounds on every side." The Great Fire of 1835 incinerated the city's financial district—the same area attacked on September 11—and is still one of New York's most horrifying disasters.

December 16, 1835, was bitterly cold; the temperature had dropped to minus 17 and a freezing gale was racing down from the north. Just before nine that evening, a gas fire broke out at Comstock & Andrews' warehouse on Merchant Street. Volunteer firemen racing to the Wall Street area were hampered by two feet of fresh snow clogging the streets. By the time they arrived, both sides of neighboring Pearl Street were ablaze.

Hydrants, wells and the East River were frozen solid. The firefighters smashed through the ice with axes, but as they pumped the water out, the wind blew it back at them. "The engines froze tight when they were not worked constantly," wrote civil engineer Charles Haswell, "and many became inactive from this cause."

As the blaze spread, all efforts to stop it proved utterly useless. "The whole fire department was so deranged and demoralized, that there was no direc- tion, and no head to give orders," noted Colonel James Hamilton. Some of the firemen drank liquor to warm themselves. The situation spiraled out of control. "The progress of the flames, like flashes of lightning, communicated in every direction," said former mayor Philip Hone, "and a few minutes sufficed to level the lofty edifices on every side."

> "A few minutes sufficed to level the lofty edifices on every side."

In this view from Brooklyn Heights of the Great Fire, twin spires of flame shoot into the night from a devastated patch of lower Manhattan.

As would happen again 166 years later, firefighters from Brooklyn, Long Island and New Jersey rushed to lower Manhattan. The intense heat from the flames melted copper roofs. Residents of Philadelphia wondered at the glow on the horizon. The domed Merchants' Exchange, considered by many the most beautiful building in the city, was, according to *The Herald,* filled with a "blazing light—a transient flood of awful glory." Offices and churches went up in smoke. No one could stop the flames, though the ingenious owner of a Broad Street oyster house saved his building by pouring buckets of vinegar onto the roof. New Yorkers carted lace, silks and shawls out of warehouses and

> ❝ **Regrets will not help us. We must act with energy, forecast and wisdom.** ❞

piled them in the streets, then watched helplessly as dancing flames reduced their goods to swirling piles of ash.

Sailors, marines and firemen tried to block the fire's progress by dynamiting buildings, and while a few of the blasts slowed some fires, others raced uninterrupted along the shore. Turpentine on an East River wharf spilled into the water and set the surface ablaze. Ships in the harbor caught fire. Sperm-oil and saltpeter warehouses exploded.

The following day "opened upon New-York with a scene of devastation around, sufficient to dismay the stoutest heart," wrote C. Foster. Stunned citizens toured a 50-acre site where 674 buildings had been destroyed, at a cost of some $20 million. "It almost made me cry to see the place where we used to worship laid waste, a mere mass of smoking ruins," recalled Catherine Burhans Wynkoop after she visited the smoldering Garden Street church.

If the size of 1835's Ground Zero was three times larger than September 11's, the death toll was far lighter. Only two people perished in what was, fortunately, a nighttime blaze in a mainly business district. So there would be many fewer funerals, much less mourning for lost loved ones, but still a daunting task of recovery to be faced. "Regrets will not help us," advised the *Evening Post.* "We must act with energy, forecast and wisdom, as becomes a brave and intelligent community."

That spirit served the city well, as it would again in 2001. The municipal government organized relief. An army of construction and demolition workers immediately began clearing debris and erecting new buildings. The stock exchange resumed trading a mere five days after the fire. As with September 11, sympathy and aid arrived from other cities and countries. New York determined to use the tragedy as impetus to build a better city. It planned an aqueduct system to bring in a reliable supply of water. Land values soared in lower Manhattan as banks and businesses rebuilt and reopened. Old Georgian- and Federal-style wood-and-brick buildings gave way to Greek Revival colossi. Many of these creations, such as the templelike Merchants' Exchange at 55 Wall Street, were built of granite using fireproof construction, and still stand today. One year later, former mayor Hone wrote of spectacular progress: "As an evidence of the prosperity of the city, the whole is rebuilt with more splendor than before."

New York, of course, continued to thrive, and its booming development turned that city into what *The Knickerbocker* magazine, in 1848, called "the Great Metropolis . . . stretching into the distance, with its domes and spires, its towers, cupolas and 'steepled chimneys.'" Within only a few years of the fire, the city, suddenly a bustling, growing metropolis of more than 300,000 people, had become the

In the picture at top left, flames engulf the beautiful, domed Merchants' Exchange. In the painting above, the raging fire has spread still farther.

country's unquestioned capital of commerce, finance and trade. One visitor from England reported that Wall Street had developed into "the most concentrated focus of commercial transactions in the world."

The city may well have been poised to become great before the fire of 1835, but that disaster did

happen, and New Yorkers responded by fighting back against fate with a fierce determination that left their city stronger than it had been. In the aftermath of September 11, with Ground Zero reclaimed ahead of schedule and many doors already reopened, there are signs that history is repeating itself. History could do much worse.

Hundreds of firefighters were lost. The NYPD lost 23 of its finest. The Port Authority Police, who patrolled the World Trade Center daily, lost 37 officers and much of its precinct, but not its resolve. Photography by James Salzano

Theirs was the largest single-day loss by any police force anywhere in the U.S., ever. Thirty-six men and one woman, working shifts for the Port Authority of New York and New Jersey, were killed on September 11. Also vanishing was a large part of the department's daily patrol—the heart of its beat—the Twin Towers. "We lost our precinct," says Chief Joseph Morris as he sits in an office filled with pictures, commemorative plaques, an artifact labeled THE FIRST FLAG FLOWN AT GROUND ZERO . . . constant reminders of the tragedy. "But we've kept our mission. We come to work every day because that's our job. It's what we do. We're the police."

Officer Raymond Murray (left, in glasses) was one who went back to work immediately after the attacks—and that is extraordinary. On the 11th, he took calls from the towers, able to offer only faint hope. "I talked to a girl four times who was up on the 106th floor. I just told her we were getting people up there as fast as possible, since at the time I thought that was the truth. In the back of my mind, I didn't know." When Murray reported for duty on the 12th, he had no idea what he would be doing. "I didn't want to sit at a security booth, I wanted to dig."

His colleague Ed Finnegan had been shot "like a hockey puck" across a corridor in the south tower during the collapse. It took him months to recover. By the time he was back in a squad car (above), the PAPD's assignment at Ground Zero was to guard the site—and to dig. "The buildings are gone and we're still here," he says. "We've got all these radios, and no calls."

BACK TO WORK

With many of its offices destroyed, the PAPD established temporary quarters in trailers on or near Ground Zero. In one of these, a shrine to fallen comrades grows day by day in front of an honor roll of the dead. (A star beside a name indicates that a positive identification has been made.) Too often, says Finnegan (below, right, conferring with Shawn Fitzpatrick), "the day doesn't move, it's just stagnant. We used to get calls for shoplifters, but now the stores are closed." During downtime some PAPD officers, including Detective Tom McHale (right), transform the rubble of Ground Zero into shields and crosses for the families of victims.

There is no such thing as an ordinary day on the job; each is filled with emotion. On September 11, Finnegan, injured, fighting through smoke after the south tower collapsed, heard a voice yelling for help, a voice he recognized. It was that of 16-year PAPD veteran Robert Vargas. The two men and others formed a chain and struggled to the street, where they were quickly on the run from the falling north tower. They dove into a building and slammed the door. Opposite and right: Back at Ground Zero months later, they are overcome by what they see—and remember. Above, at a reception for the families of victims, Finnegan comforts Sgt. Robert Kaulfers' widow, Cookie.

In June, PAPD operations shift again. For months, officers have worked a recovery site; now they patrol a construction site, dealing with injuries and handling security and crowd control. "People used to come from out of town to go to the top of the towers," says Murray. "Now it seems like three times that many come to see the hole." Some temporary booths and offices are taken down. Finnegan (below) sees life returning to "as normal as it's going to be."

The shrine is dismantled. Karl Olszewski, Frank Accardi and Finnegan gently place the honor roll aboard a truck that will transport it to Port Authority headquarters in Jersey City. Finnegan considers how different, and how difficult, the future may prove for the cops at the World Trade Center. "Everyone else went back to where they were," he says. "We're left with a hole. Two hundred and twenty floors in two buildings, and now there's just a big hole—a daily reminder of people that died." There are other reminders: Before the blackboard comes down, stars are placed next to the names of Michael Wholey and Kenneth Tietjen

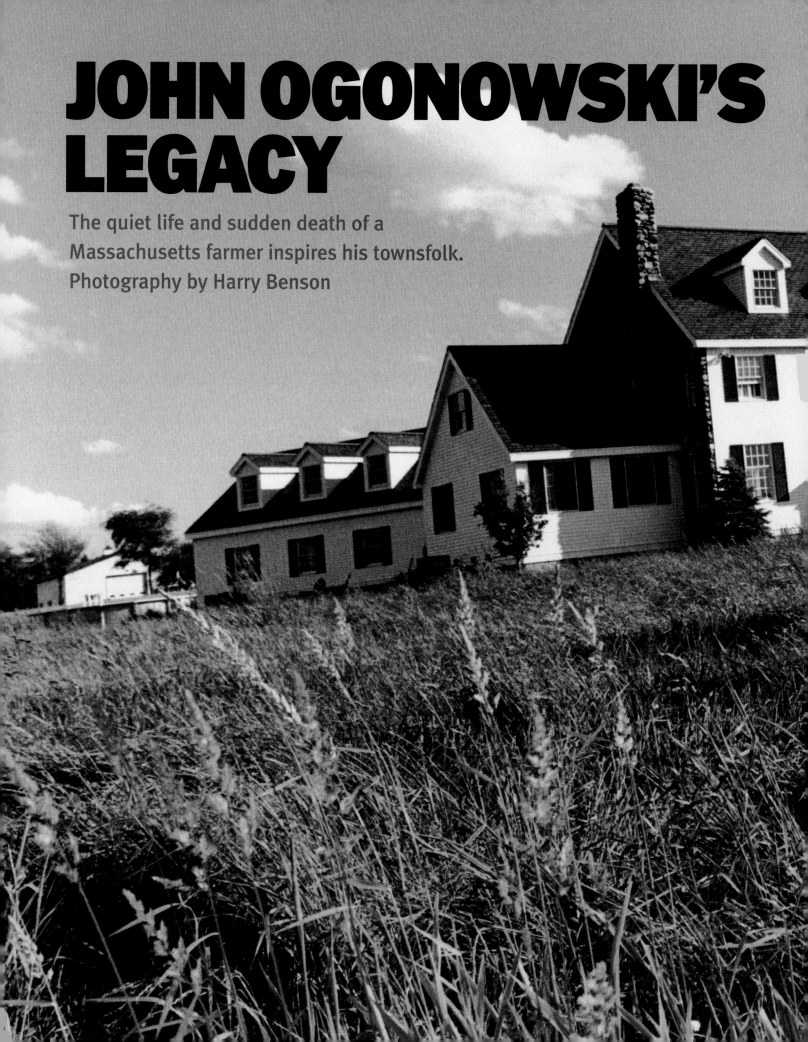

JOHN OGONOWSKI'S LEGACY

The quiet life and sudden death of a
Massachusetts farmer inspires his townsfolk.
Photography by Harry Benson

Standing in front of the house that John promised her, Peg Ogonowski finds strength in her three girls, her extended family—and in her memories of a modest and uncommonly dedicated man.

John Ogonowski, one of several farmers on Marsh Hill Road in Dracut, Mass., and latest in a line of Ogonowski farmers, rose early on September 11, drove his truck down the long gravel driveway, hung a right, passed his Uncle Albert's farm, rode down the hill and on toward Boston as the beautiful morning light intensified. He was leaving behind for two days the life that gave him self-definition—farmer, husband, father of three marvelous girls—for an alter-ego life. He served as captain with American Airlines to pay the bills, but few in Dracut thought of him as a pilot. Those who knew him at all knew him principally as the nice, quiet farmer up on Marsh Hill Road with the beautiful house and those terrific girls.

Colleen Garry, a Dracut native and the town's representative in the state legislature, heard the news later that morning and rushed to her sister's house on Lincoln Lane, just off Marsh Hill. She learned that one of the airplanes was an American jetliner and felt a sense of dread: Her cousin had recently moved up from being an American Eagle pilot to flying the big planes. "Then I heard John's name on the television," she remembers. "I turned and looked out the window and saw, right there, where John would ride his tractor, and give a little wave. He was a pilot, but I never saw him that way."

Michael Dwyer/AP

At St. Francis in Dracut on September 17, Peg, with daughter Caroline, accepts the flag. She also keeps a 767 model that American Airlines gave her, and an urn with dust from Ground Zero.

Garry and all of Dracut were about to learn much more about the soft-voiced, 50-year-old Ogonowski, who was at the helm of American Flight 11 when it took off from Logan Airport that Tuesday morning. And while towns across the land found themselves diminished in the wake of the attacks, having lost dear friends or community pillars, Dracut by contrast found itself raised up as it discovered Ogonowski's all-but-secret life. Garry, who has been energetic in getting tributes to her late townsman approved, says, "At first, we were hurt. We knew he was a good guy, and one of us, so this just wasn't fair. Then we learned more about him—he had done everything so quietly—and we realized that we had had someone in our community who really had his values straight. Then we learned even more, and realized we'd had an all-American hero in our backyard and never knew it. That was a big regret, that we didn't know him better. Once we learned about him, it seemed that continuing the good things he was doing was the best

In 1999, John Ogonowski examines produce at White Gate Farm with Sam Kong. Today, John's widow is dedicated to finding more acreage in Dracut for the Cambodians to use, though she freely admits that she is of little or no help to them as a farming consultant. "They lost their mentor in John," she says.

way of memorializing him. The land thing has gotten a big boost since September 11. The Cambodians are going to get more help. And it's all because John Ogonowski was one of us and had his head on straight and his values right."

The "land thing" and the Cambodians are intertwined, constituting the most recent chapter in the history of Ogonowskis as farmers and as people of Dracut. The Ogonowski clan first immigrated here from Poland four generations ago and settled in the Merrimack River Valley, a couple dozen miles north-

west of Boston. Today, towns much farther out are bedroom communities of the Massachusetts capital, but for most of its 300 years, Dracut has been nobody's suburb. Its main function in the 20th century was as breadbasket to Lowell, the alternately thriving and declining factory city on its southern border. Lowell's native son Jack Kerouac riffed on Dracut's vibe in his 1959 novel *Dr. Sax*: "The Dracut border wild woods surrounding Lowell."

John Ogonowski, born in 1951 in Lowell, grew up on the 125-acre Dracut farm of his parents,

"The girls keep my spirits up," says Peg. "Even if I spend all day driving them all over!" In the Ogonowski living room, before a commemorative plaque honoring their dad, Laura (left of Peg) and Caroline enjoy Mary-Kate's performance. In the backyard, Mom is drafted for a game of two-on-two.

Theresa and Alexander, along with brothers Jim and Joseph, sisters Carol and Dolores. There he learned to work—and love—the land. The farm's yield included hay, which was delivered to customers in the area, and pumpkins and corn, which would be piled high at a roadside stand during harvest.

John graduated from Keith Academy, a Catholic high school in Lowell, then went through Lowell Technological Institute, his tuition picked up by ROTC. Once in the Air Force, he piloted C-141 transports all over the world, with regular shuttles between Charleston, S.C., and Vietnam. He would ferry equipment over and, on occasion, carry bodies of American soldiers back. Upon leaving the Air Force he signed on with American Airlines in 1979. Not long thereafter he met a charming, lovely flight attendant, Peg La Valle of Bellmore, N.Y. John and Peg wed in 1983 and moved into a modest house in Pelham, just over the New Hampshire border from Dracut.

They shared their dreams with each other, dreams that began with the girls. John also wanted land—a place to farm. Peg wanted a house, and John promised he would build her one. He bought 150 acres high on Marsh Hill, just up from his uncle's place and across from the Dunlaps' farm.

The cornerstone was laid for the homestead on White Gate Farm in 1994, and as the place rose it became the talk of East Dracut. "You could tell it was a perfect house right off," says Jo Anne Fitzgerald, who works for the local weekly, *The Dispatch News.* "With the long driveway, the gates and the house, it looked like South Fork from *Dallas.*"

Peg Ogonowski, John's widow, sits in the family room of that house today and thinks back to the plans the family had. "For him, this was everything," she says. "To achieve this place, having pulled all this together at 50 years old, and having all those good years ahead of him, was very exciting to him.

"People say he was quiet, and he was, but he was not shy. He was definitely not one to talk, especially about himself, but he did what he wanted to do because he wanted to do it—and he worked very hard. He was not at all materialistic. He didn't really own anything except his dream of the farm. You look at this house and say, 'Not materialistic?' But let me tell you," she continues, laughing, "this house is all me. John, he was out in the barns."

Those barns, two pristine metal buildings just beyond the aboveground pool and the girls' basketball hoop, were Ogonowski's own playground, where he would go to unwind even at nine o'clock

In back of the house, Peg finds calm and solace—sometimes with the loyal Lily, sometimes with one of her daughters, sometimes alone.

at night after returning from a two-day swing to L.A. Surrounding them are the fields where he grew blueberries, pumpkins, peaches, corn and, mostly, hay. "He had several clients who relied on him for hay," says Peg. "His brother, Jim, has agreed to try to keep it going. One season here where the hay doesn't get cut, and this place will be a wreck. I'm concerned, of course. John and I had a clear understanding about farming: He was the farmer."

One set of tilled fields looks different than the others. Rows of Chinese water spinach, pigweed and other exotic vegetables grow beside a set of lean-tos; an overhanging shelter protects an outdoor stove and cooking utensils. "This is where the Cambodians farm," Peg says as she conducts a tour. "That greenhouse over there—John built that for them so they could plant seedlings."

The back story for this is: In the 1980s and '90s, Lowell saw a large influx of Southeast Asians and quickly found itself with a struggling underclass, many of whom were Cambodians who had fled persecution in their homeland. Various organizations sought ways to help these people, and Tufts University came up with the New Entry Sustainable Farming Project. In 1998, Ogonowski was asked if he might agree to be among farmers leasing acreage to Southeast Asians who would bring their specialized produce back to Lowell or sell it to Asian restaurants along the Eastern seaboard. Ogonowski said, "Sure, I've got some excess land we could try it on." Then, as soon as his 12 guest farmers, all of whom were taking on a second job, arrived, he went the extra mile, harrowing 15 acres, building that greenhouse, teaching American agricultural methods, hosting meetings in the big house—meantime, rarely collecting the rent.

"They're good workers," the Vietnam War veteran once said in praise of White Gate Farm's Cambodians. Pressed as to why he felt compelled to mentor as well as lease, the modest man struggled for an answer: "My family, they're all immigrants. They were farmers in their country before." His Uncle Albert explained more fully: "When my mother, John's grandmother, quit her job in the Lowell mills to move to Dracut, we got a lot of help from

the Yankee farmers here. They gave us a lot of advice and loaned us equipment, and often when we went to give it back they would tell us to keep it. Now it is our turn to help out. That's our tradition here, and John is a part of that."

"John was very proud of the Cambodians, that was good stuff," says Helen Dunlap, a teacher and heir to the farm across the road from White Gate. "You couldn't fool John—maybe you can't fool any New Englander—and he knew they were just such genuine, humble, hardworking people. He couldn't do anything else but help them."

Supporting the Cambodian farmers was one of John Ogonowski's crusades. Another was land preservation.

Dracut is a town under stress. "I would say development is our single biggest controversy," says Garry, who has watched Dracut grow from fruit stands and sandlots to a suburb of 30,000 in her lifetime. Nowhere is the development issue etched more clearly than in the beautiful countryside sur-

Dunlap (opposite, top) says if she phoned for help, John raced. "I called him 'my 911.' Isn't that eerie?" Bottom: Carol took John's cause to Washington; Jim took over his haying. Their folks (above) still live on the family farm.

rounding Marsh Hill Road. There are farms, and then there is the decade-old Surrey Lane, with its McMansions vying with McCastles. Immediately to the south of the Ogonowski and Dunlap spreads, a new 18-hole golf course is planned. The developers had originally hoped to build 239 luxury houses adjacent to their links. "John and his friends got that knocked down to 187," says Peg. "The best thing is, he got them to take the driving range out of their plans. It would have been right behind those trees. Can you imagine, with the lights? One thing

I love up here is the incredible night sky. It would have been ruined."

The golf course was a rallying point in the late 1990s for farmers and others who would preserve what remained of the town's rural character. "Helen Dunlap's late mother, Marjorie, was also the mother of open space here," says Warren Shaw Jr., a longtime Dracut selectman who operates his family's 94-year-old dairy farm. "Marjorie was the leader, John was second." In 1999, Ogonowski was a founding trustee of the Dracut Land Trust, established with the goal of preserving as much as possible of 350 acres of farmland that were at risk of sale and development, meantime working to quash or rein in the golf project. Town meetings concerning the Meadow Creek Golf Course ran as hot as things run in Dracut, Garry remembers, "until John got up to speak. He had this way about him that calmed everybody down."

That was John Ogonowski's life on September 10, 2001: family, farm, friends, some good works, a couple of causes, active in the local Veterans Administration and the Dracut Historical Society, communicant at St. Francis, evenings in his easy chair reading agriculture periodicals. On September 11 he put on his American Airlines uniform, then died either before or when his became the first plane to hit the World Trade Center. "I can't believe that he wasn't already dead," says Peg Ogonowski as she touches the folded flag presented to her during the memorial Mass at St. Francis. "They would have had to kill him to get him out of that chair."

Those were the kinds of questions that people focused on immediately after the attacks: Who were the pilots, how did the hijackers get control of the planes? In Dracut, once they had learned that the Flight 11 pilot was one of their own, GOD BLESS JOHN signs bedecked every storefront, and townsfolk often made their way up Marsh Hill to say a prayer outside White Gate Farm, where a giant American flag was draped from the outstretched arm of a large crane.

Then the story developed further; the Cambodians came into it, and the Land Trust. "Suddenly his pet causes got all this support," says reporter Bill Conlon, who tracked the story for *The Dispatch News.* "John was such a quiet, salt-of-the-earth guy, I can't help think he was looking down on the attention and acclaim with some skepticism. Of course, he would have been happy with the activity."

"Well, naturally, we felt energized by his good example," says Helen Dunlap. "We felt we had to finish what John helped to start." The Ogonowskis, even in their grief, became involved. Carol got an idea in her head about a 33-acre piece of land, long farmed by her family but not now owned by them. The parcel was adjacent to Broken Wheel Farm, home of the Okuns, Peter and Ann, who is the second cousin of John and Carol Ogonowski. The land was bought in 2000 by the golf course developer.

John Ogonowski, prior to his death, had been trying to talk the developer out of his plan to build houses there, and into, perhaps, selling the acreage for a fair price to the Land Trust. A cost of $760,000 was agreed upon, with John planning to finance a large part of the purchase himself. After his death, Carol, realizing that the Trust couldn't afford the whole nut, took a flier. She approached her U.S. Congressman, Marty Meehan. On May 31, Meehan and Sen. Ted Kennedy traveled to Dracut and promised the Ogonowskis that, somehow, the government would find funds to secure the land. "You could hear John going, 'Yes!' and see him with that twinkle in his eye," says Carol. The family hopes to place a small memorial to John in one part of the parcel, then open much of the rest for use by Cambodian farmers.

"Yes, in a sense, you can say his causes have received a boost in light of his death," says Shaw, whose farm still delivers milk in glass bottles door-to-door in Dracut. "But I'll be honest. I think even more would have been done if John was still with us. If he were here for what should have been his natural life, a lot more would have been done."

Perhaps so; in Dracut, they can never know. All they can do—and they are intent upon it—is build these living legacies, piece by piece, cause by cause.

Up on Marsh Hill Road, Peg Ogonowski looks at the proclamation signed by Meehan and Kennedy and says that she is sanguine about the attention that has come her way. "If it helps with what he was interested in, that's good," she says. "And it's good that the girls see this and are proud of their father.

"I'm so glad they're young," she continues. "They keep my spirits up. I love just walking or talking with them." She says she worries about the farm, despite Ogonowskis driving up and down the hill all day long, putting in shifts to keep up John's work. And she does have moments when she feels compelled simply to sit in the backyard and contemplate what has transpired. "Sometimes, I still can't believe it," she says. "Did that really happen? It's as if I'm daydreaming. I come out here and just stare. The whole thing has that quality of being unbelievable, literally, and I will say to myself, 'Did I just dream that?'" The view before her stretches over the hay fields to Helen Dunlap's land and, then, to the forest beyond. It's very beautiful up here, in a way John Ogonowski always understood.

RUDY GIULIANI'S YEAR

From the ashes of destruction, he rose to meet the enemy—fear—head-on. Whither now?

David Howells/Gamma

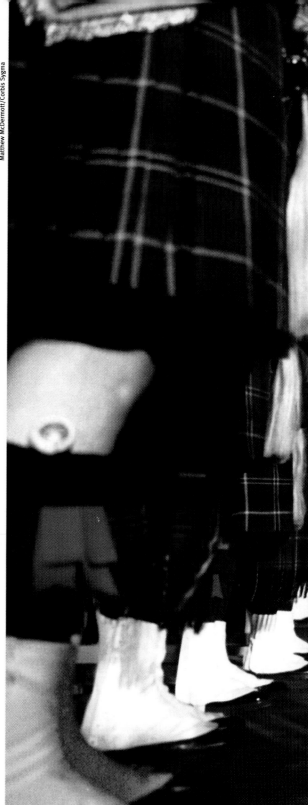

Matthew McDermott/Corbis Sygma

It is the summer of 2002, and Rudolph W. Giuliani is a busy man, running a company, giving speeches, dabbling in politics and editing his forthcoming book, much of which he wrote before September 11, called *Leadership*. It draws on lessons that he has learned about how to organize, how to manage, how to lead. One section, with a working title of "First Things First," is about "having a morning meeting every day in which you organize everything you're going to do that day, which I have been doing since 1981. That became, more or less, the organizing principle, the process by which we got through the crisis. It put everyone in the same room who had to decide and who had to give me, and the governor, information. It was decision-making in the open, as opposed to the way

Honor guards from both the police and fire departments celebrate Giuliani as he departs City Hall on his final day as mayor. He is trailed by his amour, Judith Nathan. Above, the erstwhile hizzoner enjoys the view from his new post.

a war or crisis is sometimes conducted, where the person leading it is isolated somewhere in an office, and everyone comes in and walks out and comes in and walks out. My idea had always been that the best way to make a decision is right on the battlefield, right there in the middle of it."

The former mayor of New York City is talking to LIFE in the new offices of Giuliani Partners, a con-

sulting and investment firm in midtown. The atmosphere is well-scrubbed and fortified; the man is decidedly genial. Despite recent blaring tabloid headlines on the status of his divorce proceedings with Donna Hanover, he appears rested and at ease. Of course, this is someone accustomed to confronting nasty problems. Asked how he has changed since the terrorist attacks, he says he can't yet give

an answer. "But I don't think people should answer that until they're ready. People are still going through tremendous adjustments. On a personal basis and as a country, we haven't come out of this. We're not going to really understand it till a year, two years, three years later. When John Kennedy was assassinated, it definitely had an impact on this country, but I don't think the country realized it a

Photographer Gregory Heisler and Giuliani ready themselves for a picture that will grace the cover of the *Time* 2001 Person of the Year issue.

year later—it took 10 or 12 years."

Shortly after the attacks, he walked into a room of survivors "and I saw how many families were there, and the children in their arms, and the mothers and the grandmothers. You see them all and you realize—the pain is endless. I knew from my experience with police officers, firefighters and sanitation workers dying, you can't cure the loss. But what you can do, that begins to create some calm, is say, 'You'll be financially secure.'" The charity that he

created, the Twin Towers Fund, has given away $155 million of the $175 million it has raised.

In the hours and weeks after the attack, Giuliani emerged as a paladin, able to cope with situations beyond the ken of most. *The Washington Post* called him "Winston Churchill in a Yankees cap." Former mayor Ed Koch said that Giuliani had "alienated a lot of people by being petty, but that has all been wiped out." His performance would result in his being named *Time*'s Person of the Year.

Mark Lennihan/AP

Shortly after midnight on New Year's Eve, the suddenly-ex-mayor shares the big moment with Nathan in Times Square. Below, Giuliani has just administered the oath of office to his successor, Michael Bloomberg, who has every reason to be grateful to Rudy for paving the way to City Hall.

Howard Bernstein/Bernstein & Andriulli

As January 1 approached, the day on which he would have to relinquish the office because of term limits, his luster had increased to the point where there was a grassroots campaign to extend his term by a few months, or even to change the law to grant him another term. At least some of the seed for that was sown in the mayor's office. But it wasn't meant to be, though he did get to anoint his successor, Michael Bloomberg, who rode the Giuliani bandwagon to an upset of Democrat Mark Green.

Brad Rickerby/Reuters

In February, Giuliani receives an honorary knighthood from Queen Elizabeth II. Opposite: In May, at the ceremony marking the end of the Trade Center recovery effort, he offers consolation.

On Giuliani's final day in office, he relaxed by doing five television interviews before eight a.m., going to his regular staff meeting, and attending a firefighter's funeral, a graduation ceremony for new firefighters and a ribbon-cutting at a new police station. To fill an idle moment, he rang the closing bell at the New York Stock Exchange.

Then, finally, it was on to life after the New York City mayoralty, often called the second toughest job in the country. "I'm probably busier now than when I was mayor, except for the period right after September 11," he insists. "But," he adds, "it isn't as much pressure." As CEO of Giuliani Partners, which advises on matters of security, crisis management and mergers and acquisitions, he has surrounded himself with trusted allies like former police commissioner Bernard Kerik and former fire commissioner Thomas Von Essen. His speaking engagements are frequent, often two or three a week; he reportedly earns as much as $100,000 a pop. He is working on his book. And he is active in Republican circles, advising and doing fund-raisers for such as William Simon Jr. and Jeb Bush. He is there to repay Republicans who stood up for him in the past or for candidates "who think they need my help."

So, where from here? Does he want to return to public service at some point? "I probably do, yes, but the whole experience with prostate cancer [he survived the disease in 2000 and still counsels people every week who are faced with it], which helped me a lot, gave me a perspective that my whole life was not politics, that it's much broader than just politics. I sort of have a relaxed, not fatalistic, almost religious sort of view that life takes care of itself. And right now I'm enjoying myself."

There has been widespread talk that Giuliani could become baseball commissioner or governor of New York. Will he run for President in 2004? No, he says, he will back George W. Bush, "for whom I would do almost anything. I campaigned for him even when I was undergoing radiation treatments because I felt so strongly he should be elected. And now, with the bond that I feel for him after September 11, he's my candidate. As far as what I do in politics, it probably isn't going to be for another couple of years down the road. That's when I'll refocus on public service."

This tough-as-talons politician seems genuinely comforted that "the experience I've had helps me to help other people. Having gone through hell—which is what that was, right?—and having some perspective on it, I can help people, I can help share that experience with them. And that helps me."

Says the man who will go down as New York's greatest mayor, "I have a very, very strong philosophy in how you get through life. You have to force yourself to focus on the optimistic. You have to. If you don't, something's going to take you down."

"THE WORLD WE HAVE ENTERED"

President Bush told the graduates of West Point, "You will stand between your fellow citizens and grave danger." Photography by Shannon Stapleton

On a lovely June day, in a serene setting on the Hudson River, the Commander in Chief began lightly, granting amnesty to cadets on restriction for minor offenses. Then, he turned serious: "In your last year, America was attacked by a ruthless and resourceful enemy. You graduate from this academy in a time of war." At the commencement of the U.S. Military Academy's bicentennial class, his words were forceful and emotional. "Wherever we carry it, the American flag will stand not only for our power, but for freedom," he said. "Our nation's cause has always been larger than our nation's defense. We fight, as we always fight, for a just peace—a peace that favors human liberty. We will defend the peace against threats from terrorists and tyrants . . . In the world we have entered, the only path to safety is the path of action. And this nation will act."

The cadets cheered when the President cast the fight as one "between good and evil," but these strong-minded young people shed tears when he backed up that claim: "Moral truth is the same in every culture, in every time, and in every place. Targeting innocent civilians for murder is always and everywhere wrong. Brutality against women is always and everywhere wrong."

Flags fluttered in the breeze from the river, and then nearly a thousand hats flew into the sky. The Army's newest group of leaders hugged one another and their parents, then set off to meet the foe.

All photographs: Gamma

INTO AFGHANISTAN

Jim Hollander/Reuters

Brennan Linsley/Reuters/Landov

America and its allies root out a terrorist enemy, and along the way free an oppressed people.

Shortly after the United States was stunned by the September 11 acts of terrorism, President George W. Bush declared war. The U.S. response would involve "every resource at our command." Speaking at the National Cathedral on September 14, he said, "War has been waged against us by stealth and deceit and murder. This nation is peaceful, but fierce when stirred to anger. This conflict . . . will end in a way, at an hour, of our choosing."

Each modern war differs from the one that preceded it. This may be a matter of technical advances, of duration, or of terrain, but each is singular. "Even the vocabulary of this war will be different," said Secretary of Defense Donald Rumsfeld. "When we 'invade the enemy's territory,' we may well be invading his cyberspace. There may not be as many beachheads stormed as opportunities denied." Said Secretary of State Colin Powell: "We're not fighting an enemy that is located on a battlefield where we all can see the enemy and just

go after him. This is an enemy that intends to remain hidden. It's a very resourceful enemy."

So, a new war, this time waged against terrorism, and while there was plenty to contend with at home, once again Americans would have to go to a faraway place to defend democracy. In this endeavor, the U.S. forged a coalition of scores of countries to provide military and financial support.

On October 7, 2001, the U.S. and Great Britain, its most active partner, launched military strikes in Afghanistan against the Taliban, the ultraconservative faction that emerged in the mid-'90s after Soviet troops had withdrawn. By 2001 the Taliban—which excluded women from jobs or education, destroyed non-Islamic relics and employed draconian measures of punishment—controlled all but a small part of northern Afghanistan. This made the country an ideal haven for al-Qaeda, the Islamic terrorist sect formed in the late 1980s by Osama bin Laden. This well-funded organization has slain and maimed thousands in the past decade. In February 1998, al-Qaeda stated that it was the duty of all Muslims to kill U.S. citizens and their allies everywhere. This group launched the September

As they enter Afghanistan, U.S. special ops soldiers man the rear of a Chinook helicopter. Opposite: A Navy Hornet departs the carrier *Carl Vinson*.

Carolyn Cole/Los Angeles Times (2)

Pete Souza/Chicago Tribune

Many Taliban were captured and held prisoner (left). Still others were turned and went on to fight with the Northern Alliance, like 16-year-old Sadeq (top left), who is leading his sheep on the arduous march to the front. Above, an Alliance soldier watches the fury of a B-52 bomb strike near Rabat.

11 attacks. Now the Taliban and al-Qaeda were in the crosshairs. By December, coalition forces and the Northern Alliance, a diverse Afghan collection of anti-Taliban political parties and ethnic groups, had driven the Taliban from the country. Much of the muscle for this effort came from heavy U.S. air strikes, particularly from the B-1B long-range bomber and F/A-18 Hornets launched from carriers in the Arabian Sea.

Still, there was no sign of bin Laden. Asked if he wanted the al-Qaeda leader dead, Rumsfeld replied, "Oh, my goodness gracious yes . . . you bet your life." Spy satellites scanned the country and aerial surveillance was enhanced by a new unmanned craft called the Global Hawk, which can fly all day

at 60,000 feet and features remarkable imaging equipment. And now it was time for the ground forces, who had to go into the mountains and caves to check out the intelligence gathered from above. On March 2, Operation Anaconda sent 2,000 U.S., Afghan and coalition troops into a rugged area of eastern Afghanistan. Hundreds of al-Qaeda fighters were killed.

In April it was disclosed that a bounty of $100,000 had been offered for the capture of any coalition soldier, and $50,000 for the body of a dead one. Still the allied operations continued, with names like Ptarmigan, Snipe and Condor, which was a weeklong mission in May that sought out fighters who had brought down heavy gunfire on

Australian troops.

Beginning in the spring, the emphasis was on special operations teams deployed to ferret out small bands of Taliban and al-Qaeda fighters. American, British and Australian commandos hunted high and low in a counterinsurgency campaign but found no large numbers of the enemy. This suggested that they had been driven to remote mountain areas or into neighboring Pakistan.

The result of all this is that Afghanistan is now essentially free to re-create itself. This will not be easy. Tribal and cultural groups are holding a *loya jirga,* a traditional conclave to select an interim government, with the hopes of a general election by the end of 2003. But there are so many schisms along ethnic, religious and political lines that unified agreement will be difficult. And, of course, discord will continue to be sown by Taliban and al-Qaeda survivors. As long as they are on the run, however, always looking back over their shoulder, it will be harder for them to mount and execute the more sophisticated acts of terrorism.

This war continues to fester. Not long ago, a slogan appeared on a wall in Kandahar: JIHAD. DEATH TO AMERICA. And the war will not end at the border of Afghanistan. The relentless pursuit of terrorists across the globe by America and at least some of its allies has only just begun.

After the Taliban were routed, Afghans were again free to savor the fruits of liberty. Above, eight-year-old Najibe during a school session. The Taliban didn't permit females to attend school or hold a job. Even the simpler indulgences, like listening to music or taking a shave, are a source of delight.

DAN ROWAN'S WAY WEST

A New York City firefighter, emotionally rent by September 11, finally had to take flight. His catharsis was found on a coast-to-coast odyssey, embarked upon to thank America—and to heal his own battered spirit. Photograph by Henry Groskinsky

Ladder 9 and Engine 33 share a firehouse in lower Manhattan. On September 11 they lost 10 men. Dan Rowan of Ladder 9, distraught, worked at Ground Zero for a month, then became a liaison to victims' families. He handled arrangements for firefighters' funerals, work that affected him deeply, in good ways and bad. While grieving daily, he was heartened by constant kindness. Because the FDNY was stretched thin, firefighters from across the land came to fill out honor guards at the services. "One guy dies and we have 10,000 of us, as far as the eye can see," says Rowan. "But with five, six memorials a day . . ." He wondered how he could thank the selfless volunteers. One day, a homeless man walked into the firehouse and offered Rowan all that he had, $1.22. That was the catalyst. Rowan decided to go, to get on a bike and thank the firefighters who had lent support—and to thank America itself

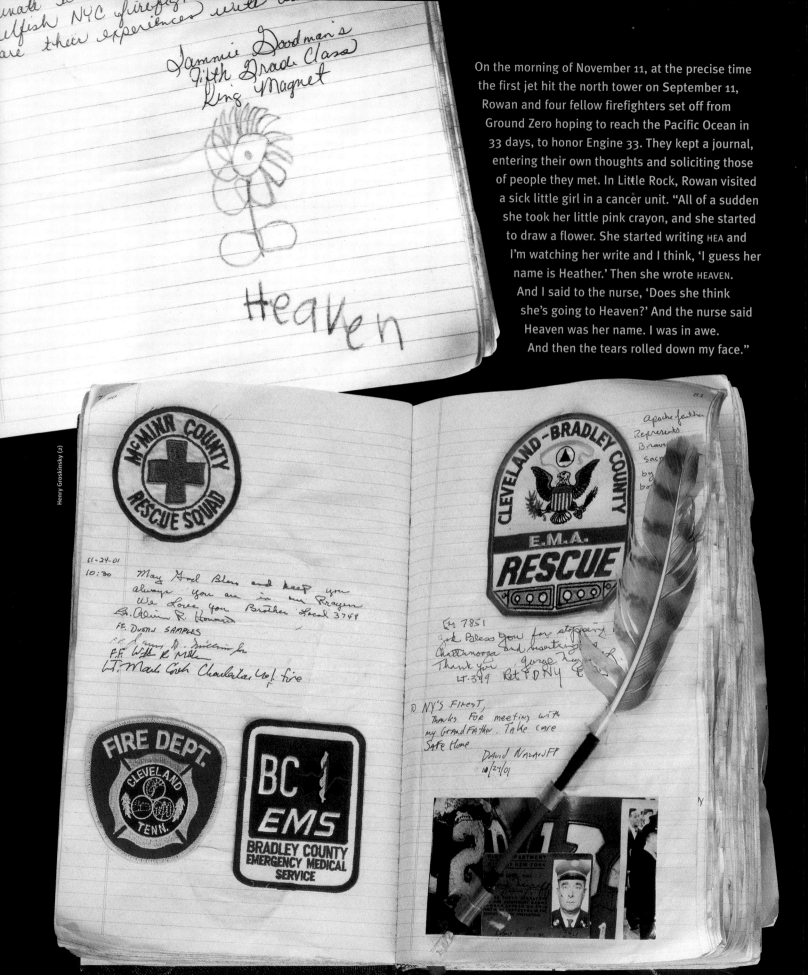

On the morning of November 11, at the precise time the first jet hit the north tower on September 11, Rowan and four fellow firefighters set off from Ground Zero hoping to reach the Pacific Ocean in 33 days, to honor Engine 33. They kept a journal, entering their own thoughts and soliciting those of people they met. In Little Rock, Rowan visited a sick little girl in a cancer unit. "All of a sudden she took her little pink crayon, and she started to draw a flower. She started writing HEA and I'm watching her write and I think, 'I guess her name is Heather.' Then she wrote HEAVEN. And I said to the nurse, 'Does she think she's going to Heaven?' And the nurse said Heaven was her name. I was in awe. And then the tears rolled down my face."

Henry Groskinsky (2)

The cyclists rode through Virginia— Manassas, Lynchburg, Bristol—and into the hills of Tennessee, meeting with brethren along the way. "You're born a firefighter," says Rowan. "It's the same circus everywhere. You really have to have a kind of craziness to run into a fire. So we would meet these guys, and it was just like you've known them forever."

"Pampa was the smallest town with the largest heart you'd ever want to see," says Rowan of the Texas whistle-stop. The Pampa firefighters hosted the New Yorkers at a spaghetti dinner, and the next morning cooked up a mess of eggs and sausage, biscuits and gravy. Below, Pampa fireman Jesse Hanes leads an escort, as locals line Route 60 to wish the cyclists Godspeed on the road to Amarillo.

The cyclists find a windbreak behind the trucks of the Blythe, Calif., fire department. "I'll never pedal east to west again," says Rowan. "The prevailing winds killed us." But the quintet fought through to Pasadena, where Rowan's daughters Chelsea, eight, and Caitlin, 12, were on hand to greet Dad. "I missed my family an awful lot," says Rowan, "but I'd go out tomorrow and do the exact same thing."

SURVIVORS REVISITED

Theirs were some of the faces of Ground Zero. Today they stand as profiles in courage. Photography by Joe McNally

In the immediate aftermath of September 11, longtime LIFE photographer Joe McNally holed up in a studio in southern Manhattan and began creating a document, a dignified tribute to those directly affected by events at Ground Zero. Over the course of two weeks, scores of people—survivors, firefighters, police officers, volunteers, doctors, nurses, widows, children, desperate searchers in the rubble—came before the lens of a 12-foot by 16-foot by 12-foot Polaroid and bared their souls. The camera takes pictures that are 40 inches wide by 80 inches tall—larger than life-size—and yields images of striking immediacy and clarity. McNally hoped his portraits might reveal the person within. The resonance of these pictures became immediately evident when some two dozen of them first appeared, in smaller size, in the LIFE book *One Nation.* An exhibit of 50 of the images drew record

Joanne Foley Gross and brother Danny Foley stand on the Pine Bush, N.Y., site where they will build a cabin to house possessions of the late Tommy Foley.

crowds when it traveled to public spaces in six U.S. cities and in London. Those photographs and 25 others are to be displayed on the mall of New York City's Rockefeller Center in 2002 to commemorate the one-year anniversary—and the people—of September 11.

LIFE's editors have repeatedly been asked in the past several months, "What ever happened to the guy with the squeegee?" and "Did that fellow recover from his burns?" The editors wondered if, by revisiting several subjects whose stories were extraordinarily compelling, something of value might be learned about resilience and coping. McNally and journalist Melissa Stanton accepted the assignment and came back with a new document, this one about the passage of time, wounds healing (if slowly), lives forever changed, perseverance. These six individuals do not—cannot—stand in for the many others in the *Faces of Ground Zero* project, or for the many thousands of others affected by September 11. Everyone copes in a personal way. But what these six can represent is the power of courage and resolve in the face of tragedy.

Joanne Foley Gross 35

Sister of late FDNY firefighter Tommy Foley

Her brother Tommy Foley, 32, a 10-year FDNY veteran and a part-time model and actor, was finishing his shift at Rescue 3 when the attacks occurred. He was killed in the south tower. Ten days later, Gross's husband, K.C., a Mount Vernon, N.Y., firefighter, and her other brother, Danny, an FDNY firefighter, found Tommy's body amid the debris at Ground Zero.

" Life has changed dramatically. I quit my job as a mortgage broker because I didn't want to be dealing with anybody's small problems anymore—closing dates and things like that. I had enough responsibility with having to worry about my parents and my brother, my three children and husband. They've become my job. I've reprioritized. My kids are young and they are what's important. I need to focus on what's important.

Every step we take these days is taken with Tommy in mind. There has been a lot to do, whether it's returning calls, filling out documents, writing thank-you notes. I'm the administrator of his estate, so I do the paperwork, which I want to do because when it stops, I won't be helping my brother anymore.

Sometimes, it's very hard to get through the day. I think about Tommy all the time. I think about my kids, and how Tommy was my son K.C.'s godfather. K.C. is eight and is having trouble dealing with death and losing his uncle, whom he idolized.

I know I look at life differently now. I try not to take anything for granted, not to sweat the small stuff. I take the time now to treasure what's important, and I try to live life how it should be lived, instead of wasting it away. We're here for such a short time.

My brother did so much in his life. Tommy was a firefighter, he rode bulls in rodeos, appeared on *The Sopranos* and *Third Watch,* modeled, trained his dog to be a champion bird dog. He did more in his 32 years than a 100-year-old person, and although his life was short, it had such purpose. Tommy was bigger than life, and we realize this even more so now. He kept in touch with everyone and made an impact on so many. We know of three couples who have named babies after Tommy. He amazed us when he was here, and he continues to amaze us. "

Danny Foley 29

Firefighter, FDNY, Ladder 49 (formerly of Engine 68)
Brother of late FDNY firefighter Tommy Foley

Off duty on September 11, he rushed to the scene to search for his brother, Tommy, and other firefighters. Afterward, in addition to working at his Bronx firehouse, Foley toiled on his own time at Ground Zero until the recovery efforts ended.

" I wouldn't leave the fire department for the world, but it's more difficult now. It's that you're scared something's going to happen. It's because you're constantly around it. At the firehouse, guys are talking about it—it's the topic of conversation every minute of every day. You never get away from it. Not that I want to get away from it, but it's difficult to never get a break.

Everybody in the firehouse knows 40 or 50 guys, or more, who were killed. We're all hurting and are trying to help each other. When I come home, I have to be there for my family. It's been a difficult year, but I don't take anything for granted anymore. I live each day as if it could be my last one. I try to enjoy my family and my friends. You've got to cherish those things.

I've always had a close family, even prior to the 11th, but we're even closer now. Unfortunately, Tommy's not here with us. One thing I've realized is that Tommy affected many people. It's unbelievable, the people who have written to us about how he affected their lives. Tommy had a special quality, and everybody, everywhere he went, remembered him. I try to use that now, use him as a role model for how I'd like to live my life. "

Jan Demczur 48
Window Washer

When the plane struck Tower No. 1, Demczur and five others became trapped in an elevator 50 floors up. Demczur pried open the door with his squeegee. Faced with a wall of plasterboard, he went at it with the metal blade of his wiper. All of the trapped took turns and finally made a one-foot-by-18-inch hole. They crawled out, astonishing firefighters. The escape took 95 minutes.

" I can't talk about it. "

Jan Demczur 49
Window washer

Moments after the first plane hit, Jan Demczur became trapped with five other men in a smoke-filled elevator in Tower 1. Using his window-washing tools, Demczur and the men wedged open the elevator doors and chipped at three layers of Sheetrock until they broke through to a bathroom on the 50th floor. They escaped within minutes of the tower's collapse. Since then, Demczur, a native of Poland, has been featured by media throughout the world; in April, he was feted in Washington, D.C., where he donated his uniform and squeegee to the Smithsonian Institution. Demczur, who lives in Jersey City, N.J., directly across the Hudson River from Ground Zero, says he is still too fearful to return to work.

" A doctor who examined me that day told me to see my primary-care doctor the next day, which I did because I couldn't stop shaking. The Red Cross set me up in group counseling with other people who had been at the World Trade Center. I went to that and to personal counseling. I'm told I have post-traumatic stress. I haven't been able to drive since September 11. My hands shake. I get dizzy. I'm trying to get over that. My wife does all the driving now, but I need to be able to drive. I'm a different person than I used to be. Before September 11, I was smart. If I wanted to do something, I could do it. I was able to give people advice. Now when I need to do something, I start it, then don't finish. I go down to my basement and forget the reason I went there. I'm distracted. My brain is working slow.

In the first two months I had nightmares, not so much now. At one point I thought maybe we should move, maybe go to Poland. But when my children, who are 14 and 11, heard I was thinking of selling the house, they said no. They like it here. Some-

times they do ask, 'When are you going to go to work?' I tell them, 'I'm still not fit to work.' I explain that a lot of people are in shock and can't work, and maybe can't work for the rest of their lives. I tell them some people go on disability, some retire early, some do different work, and some get cuckoo because the brain doesn't accept what happened.

I know that no part of my body was hurt. I know there are so many people who lost their lives, and people who lost their families. Women died who were pregnant, 343 firemen were lost, so many policemen and others who were trying to help. I was there in 1993, when the bomb exploded. I was on the third floor that day. I felt the shaking and saw all the smoke. I evacuated safely, helped other people on the street and the next day started working in the cleanup. But this time was different. This time changed my life. I'm not the same anymore.

I've only been to the World Trade Center once since September 11. My wife wanted us to go. We went in December. Pictures were still there of people who were missing. People I knew. **"**

Katrina Marino 36

Wife of late FDNY firefighter Kenneth Marino

Katrina Marino last saw her husband, Kenny, at 8:15 a.m. on September 11 when she and their children, Kristin, now four, and Tyler, two, stopped at his firehouse for an unexpected visit before heading to a Manhattan appointment. A half hour later, Kenny Marino, 40, was on his way to the World Trade Center. Along with 10 others from Rescue 1, he perished in the north tower. His body was not found.

Katrina Marino 35
Wife of missing firefighter Kenneth Marino of Rescue 1, pictured with daughter Kristin, 3, and son Tyler, 1
Eleven firefighters from Rescue 1 responded to alarms. None returned.
"Kenny was listed as injured and I was very hopeful, but later they said it was a mistake. I try not to get upset in front of the kids. I need to be there for them. My daughter has been an inspiration. It came to the point where I had to tell her Daddy's in heaven. She said, 'Don't worry, Mommy, you've got me and Tyler.'"

FACES OF GROUND ZERO LIFE 167

" That morning, when the kids and I were leaving the firehouse, Kenny went around the car and kissed each of us goodbye. I remember thinking that was so nice, because he could have just leaned over. In retrospect, it's so important that he made sure to give each of us a good kiss.

Later, when I had to tell Kristin that Daddy was not coming home, I found out that during our visit he had promised to bring her a *Wizard of Oz* prize. After three weeks she was still talking about it, so I took a Dorothy doll that I had bought for Christmas and put it in the trunk of Kenny's car. When I opened the trunk and she saw it, she was so excited, 'Daddy didn't forget my prize!' I had bought other toys, so I said, 'Look, Daddy bought the Scarecrow for Tyler!' Those became their dolls from Daddy. Then Kristin said to me, 'Daddy got you a prize too.' Chills went through me. I asked her, 'What did Daddy get me?' She said, 'Are you going to cry if I give it to you?' I said, 'Is it okay if I cry?' She said no. So I told her, 'I think I'll be so happy, I'm not going to cry.' She went into her room and came out with a Santa Claus fireman ornament. I had never seen it before. She told me, 'Daddy bought this for you.' So we each have a present from Kenny. If I ever start to cry, which I have really tried not to do in front of them, Kristin says, 'Remember, Mommy, the prize from Daddy.' To her, that prize means I should be happy.

Even though I was always the main part of my kids' lives because Kenny was at work, now it's just me. What really hurts is not seeing him come through the door. I always looked forward to Kenny coming home. In a way, he is still here. All his things are here. I'm not throwing anything out. Everything that was Kenny's is a memory. We talk about him a lot, and Tyler still cries for his father. He was only one and a half when it happened, but he was so close to Kenny. I explained it all to him by saying, 'Daddy got a big, big boo-boo and went up to heaven.' But every fire truck he sees, he says 'Dada, Dada.' The holidays were hard because Kenny was Mr. Holiday himself. He decorated everything. He did the Easter baskets. He stuffed the Christmas stockings, especially mine. No one will love our kids or me as much as Kenny did.

It has been sinking in more for all of us lately. In the beginning there were people in and out of our house helping—charities offered us chances to go to shows—so we kept busy, busy, busy. There are eight firefighter widows in our area, and I've gotten together with them for dinner a few times. It's been therapeutic. Spending time with them helps because we're all in the same boat. Another change has been our financial situation. When Kenny was alive, we were barely getting by. He barely cleared $1,100 per paycheck every other week. An entire paycheck went to pay our mortgage. Firefighters all have to work other jobs, and Kenny always worked a couple of side jobs. We struggled so hard. The sad thing is, now I get his pension. I get his whole pay tax-free. Now I can buy what we need, but Kenny's not here to enjoy these things with me. I call it our 'sad money.' Firefighters risk their lives every day. They don't get paid well for it, but they get it when they die. What's fair about that? "

Manu Dhingra 28

Formerly a securities trader at Andover Brokerage

When the first airliner crashed into the north tower, Dhingra's elevator was just arriving on the 83rd floor. Fire shot down on either side of the elevator shaft. Burned over nearly 40 percent of his body, he made his way down a stairwell to the lobby. He was released from New York City's Weill Cornell Burn Center on October 2.

66 When I was in the hospital that first day, I asked a nurse how my friends were. She told me the buildings had fallen. I knew then that even if just one person had died, I had no right to feel sorry for myself. It's hard to remind myself every day, but I try to, that considering the alternative, I am privileged to have the scars and burns. I'll have scars forever, but I think of them as my medals for walking down those 83 flights of stairs.

After the hospital, I returned to my apartment. For some reason, I didn't want to leave Manhattan. Even now, it's hard to leave the city. Here, we're all kind of healing together, which feels comfortable. It is very scary here, but also very comfortable.

People think once you get out of the hospital you are well. But my parents came to help pretty much every day, and I had a nurse coming to my home for a month. I had six months of rehab and gradually got back the mobility in my hands. I don't

have pain now, just discomfort, but I still wear nylon pressure garments. Because I have to be careful not to be in sunlight, I mostly stay inside. I've had support from family and friends, even strangers. That has really helped. I've received countless cards, including a lot from little kids. I was in India recently, where I was born, and it made me think about how life has such value in the United States. If I had

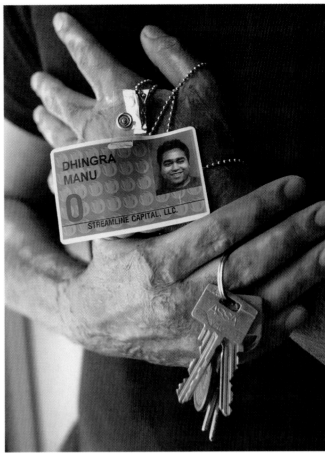

to get hurt somewhere in the world, I'm glad that it was in America. People here care about life.

I've tried not to look back, just ahead. I was never angry, not even at the terrorists. That day they took away so much from me, and from everybody else, that I refuse to give them any more attention. That would just make them more important. I'm really trying to put that day behind me.

As difficult as the experience has been, it has also been exciting. It has shown me a side of myself I would have never seen. I'm happy with who I am right now. When I was a trader, I would think, 'Oh, I wish my life was this. I wish I had that.' But when I was lying in the hospital, the only thing I wanted back was my life, nobody else's. I did the work I did for financial reasons, but now I look at how precious time is. I think of all those people who aren't with us anymore, many of whom had great jobs and lots of money, and who would give up all that money just to be here. I don't want to go back to what I was doing. I feel I have a duty to find something to do with my life that is really fulfilling and that I love.

I still see a psychologist every week. It helps to be able to talk about things. Even though I feel lucky to be alive, I do look in the mirror and see these scars. I'm fearful of a lot of things now: flying, tall buildings. I don't know if that will ever change, but I try to tackle my fears. What's worse than dying is not being able to live. I can't let the terrorists win. I have to get out and get on with my life—in part because I know there are 3,000 people who would trade places with me in a heartbeat. ”

Louie Cacchioli 51
Firefighter, Engine 47
Rescued many from Tower No. 1

66 I stepped outside after
bringing about 40 or 50 people
down a stairway. I looked around.
It was crazy. Somebody yelled,
'Look out! The tower's coming
down!' I started running. I tossed
my air mask away to make myself
lighter. Next thing I know, there's
a big black ball of smoke. I threw
myself on my knees, and I'm
crying. I said to myself, 'Oh, my
God, I'm going to die.' I was
crawling. Then—the biggest
miracle thing in the world. My
hands came onto an air mask. It
still had air. Another 15 seconds,
I wouldn't have made it. 99

FACES OF GROUND ZERO

Louie Cacchioli 52

Firefighter, FDNY, Engine 47, now retired

**On September 11, Cacchioli, a veteran of two
decades with the FDNY, became trapped with
another firefighter in an elevator on the 24th
floor of the north tower. After prying open the
doors, the men lost each other in the smoke.
Cacchioli led as many as 40 civilians down a
stairwell. Then the tower fell, leaving him
choking in dust and debris.**

66 I'm dealing with it, I'm living with it, but I
have a lot of guilt. Tommy Hetzel of Ladder
13—I kept him with me in the elevator because as
a ladder guy he had tools that engine guys like me
didn't have. He never made it out. A young fellow
on detail duty that I had relieved at the firehouse,
Matt Barnes. Instead of going home he went to the
World Trade Center with his own company. If I had
not relieved him until later, he wouldn't have been
able to go down there. But I relieved him early, and
he's gone too. His house, Ladder 25, lost six guys.
I was very lucky. God directed me to make split-
second decisions that took me the right way every-
place I went. What bothers me also is that I got five
chances that day in close calls. Some of my buddies
didn't even get one. We're all in there to do our jobs,
so why should I get more chances than them? People I've met since then have told me I'm a hero.

I tell them, 'Listen, I am not a hero. It was my job. This is what I got paid to do.' I've been on this job 20 years, and I've never considered myself a hero. To me, the heroes are the 343 firefighters we lost down there. Those are my heroes because they stayed in there. They didn't have the opportunities I had, the chances I had to get out.

So why am I here? I don't know.

But I know I've got to move on. Like somebody told me, 'Louie, we lost a lot, but just remember one thing, you have a lot to live for. Look at your family.' I do have a great family. If it weren't for my wife and kids, I probably would've blown my brains out months ago. They're what keep me going.

I haven't worked since the 11th. After that day, I went down digging for five or six days in a row. I was possessed. I felt guilty being home, I had to be there. But we didn't find one survivor. Not one. After six days of digging, I couldn't talk. I'd lost my voice because I wasn't wearing a mask. My lungs were shot. I couldn't see right. And I wasn't one of the worst ones—there were people there in worse shape than me. My wife took me to the throat doctor, who, before even sitting me down said, 'Louie, you're going right to the pulmonary doctor.' I did. He put me on medical leave and told me, 'You've got lung damage, you've got eye damage. You can never be a firefighter again.' I started crying like a baby. Being a firefighter was what I lived for. I loved my job.

My official last day on the job was February 28. Months later, I was still waiting for my disability pay. I had to take a loan to support my family. That was okay. I don't really care about money now. My priorities are completely different than before. I don't have too many bad days. If I get upset about something, I just flash back a little bit and think, 'Are you kidding? This is going to bother you after what you went through?' Then I just go on.

I thought I'd seen everything in 20 years in my Harlem firehouse. I've seen people jump, I've seen people burnt. I've seen bodies that have been stabbed, shot. But it was all nothing compared to September 11. I worry about more terrorism. I worry about everything. I'm going for counseling. I have to go. I didn't think I needed it at first, but I did. I can talk about it now. I had cried for 70-something days in a row, but time does heal things. We'll never forget, but we've got to go on. And hopefully, we'll never see a day like that again. **"**

New York City

On September 11, four passenger jets departed within 45 minutes of one another from three East Coast airports. Two from Boston pierced the Twin Towers, causing their collapse. The death toll in Manhattan was 2,825. Recovery efforts finished ahead of schedule, and rebuilding has begun.

HALLOWED GROUND

In three different states, three different sites of destruction and recovery are united by a date—September 11—and also by a name. Here is one man's view of places known forevermore as Ground Zero. Photography by Denis Waugh

Pennsylvania

A United flight from Newark traveled as far west as Akron before changing its heading. Passengers, alerted to the New York attacks through cell-phone conversations, stormed the cockpit. The plane plunged toward a wooded section of Somerset County and crashed in a field, killing all 45 aboard.

Arlington, Virginia

A flight from Washington Dulles Airport also reached Ohio before reversing its course. Fighter planes were unable to intercept the jetliner, which struck the Pentagon, killing 64 aboard and 125 in the building. Here, too, recovery proceeds apace. A sign counts the seconds to September 11, 2002.

Independence Days
Remembrance and Reflection

In the fall of 2001, LIFE asked some very fine writers to share their thoughts regarding September 11. They did so—eloquently—in the book ONE NATION. In the summer of 2002 we again approached several of the country's eminent historians, novelists, essayists and poets with a proposition. We asked each to view their Fourth of July through the prism of September 11. What had happened? What was the state of our liberty? The reports arrived from Lawrence, Kans., and Chautauqua, N.Y.; from New Orleans and New Hampshire; from Chicago and Washington, D.C.; from the Pacific Northwest and Manhattan; from England and Italy. They are often poignant, sometimes angry or funny, uniformly heartfelt. Wending our way to David McCullough, at the parade in Martha's Vineyard, Mass., we begin with a provocative dispatch by James Bradley from Bass Lake, Wisc.

I nnocent civilians in buildings in the nation's largest city. Suddenly, terror airmen from out of the blue snuffed out their lives. The nation was horrified.

An enemy attack on soldiers in battle is one thing, but an enemy attack on unsuspecting civilians is a cowardly act, beyond the pale. So when some enemy combatants were later captured, they were held incommunicado. Their names were not even released to the Red Cross as required by the Geneva Convention. Interrogations went far beyond "name, rank and serial number." Few of the nation's people complained. Our nation faces an evil threat, everyone agreed. This is a different kind of war, the leaders explained. A clear majority agreed that those who stooped to kill innocent civilians without warning should be shown no mercy.

The year was 1942.

On Saturday, April 18, 1942, 80 American Doolittle Raiders shocked Tokyo with a daylight bombing raid. While attacking their military targets, American airplane gunners also killed children in schoolyards and bombed patients in their hospital beds. Shocked by these "evil" deeds, the outraged people of Japan demanded revenge. Japanese patriotism glowed white-hot. Japan captured some of the Raiders and did not release their names.

Holding American Prisoners of War incommunicado and not even informing their mothers of their whereabouts was clearly against the Geneva Convention. Demanding more from a POW than his name, rank and serial number also contravened the rules of war. The people of America, from President Roosevelt on down, condemned Japan's illegal actions against helpless prisoners as "barbaric" and against the norms of civilized behavior.

My father was one of the boys who later raised the American flag on the Japanese island of Iwo Jima. He and his buddies fought against a totalitarian government that not only trampled upon the human rights of prisoners but also those of

its own people. Japanese government authorities held Japanese citizens incommunicado in jails, with no legal representation. American boys like my dad fought to defend their country, a country governed by the rule of law. Even in the midst of WWII—history's single most horrific slaughter—Franklin Roosevelt did not hold American citizens in jails incommunicado. And FDR was stern and fair even with enemies who had wished and worked for America's destruction. This wheelchair-bound President made sure foreign POWs in American camps watched first-run movies.

Today we Americans feel threatened. We characterize the enemy as "evildoers." We are distraught over the many New York–area children robbed of their fathers and mothers.

The attack unifies us. Our leaders explain that this is a different kind of war. We are asked to give up some of our freedoms in the interest of "homeland security." But America in peril is nothing new. The first President who informed America they were involved in "a different kind of war" was not from Texas, but Hyde Park, New York.

Is our homeland security more threatened now than it was in World War II? Do the plots of the current "evildoers" put the safety of our civilians in greater jeopardy than the plans of our enemies 60 years ago?

Hardly. Millions of enemy soldiers had conquered much of the globe back then. Rockets rained down on Londoners' heads. By the time Pearl Harbor brought us into the war, tens of millions of people all over Mother Earth had perished violently. On December 8, 1941, the Library of Congress shipped a box from Washington to Ft. Knox, for safekeeping. The box contained the original Declaration of Independence, Constitution and Bill of Rights.

The Germans and Japanese killed more American civilians in the opening months of WWII than died in the World Trade Center. A Japanese submarine shelled a Santa Barbara oil refinery. American flyboys sank another Japanese sub in waters near Seattle on Christmas Eve, 1941. Four months after Pearl Harbor, on the evening of April 10, 1942, thousands of Americans stood on the Jacksonville, Fla., beach, horrified by what they saw out there in the dark Atlantic. A German U-boat (U-123) was visible. Flames illuminated it. The flames were from burning oil. Oil seeping from the torpedo hole in the hull of the just-sunk U.S. civilian oil tanker, the Gulfamerica. (Incidentally, the Gulfamerica had no insurance coverage. No insurance company in the world would insure an American oil tanker.)

Nazi subs sank 397 American ships just off our shores; most of them were clearly civilian vessels with civilians aboard. Over 5,000 American civilians died just off the homeland at the hands of German U-boats operating in our coastal waters. Children across America lost parents.

On this July Fourth, it is important to reflect that America triumphed in two important ways in World War II. Historians have well documented our impressive military victories. But we also triumphed as a people by maintaining our respect for the rule of law. We were able to turn back the greatest threat in our history without trampling on the rights guaranteed in the Constitution.

Yes, regrettably, we removed Japanese Americans from the West Coast, but many of their sons, having proved their loyalty to the United States, were free to walk out of the camps and join the U.S. Army. Schools operated in the camps, as did a free press. No one was held incommunicado. And my father's generation later apologized for this act that was so contrary to the American Spirit.

We as a nation are only as free as the least among us. If our government can do something to one of us, it can do it to all of us. On this July Fourth, two American citizens—(Abdullah al Muhajir, the former Jose Padilla, and Yasser Esam Hamdi)—are in an American jail, denied access to attorneys by our American government. POWs—sons of mothers—are being held secretly at an American military base. Reportedly, the United States of America is having some tortured by cooperative allied countries. Someday my son or your daughter may be a POW in a foreign jail. They may well be considered "evil" by their captors. From what moral high ground will we be able to demand their fair treatment? Will a future evil enemy who is torturing my screaming son Jack laugh about obeying laws? Will he taunt bleeding Jack, "Why didn't America obey its own laws back then?"

Islamic terrorists first bombed the World Trade Center on February 26, 1993. Six people were killed. One thousand more were injured. Six suspects were arrested and charged. Their names were released to the press and they had access to legal representation.

All six of the 1993 World Trade terrorists were found guilty and each was sentenced to 240 years in prison. Each. The world-class American justice system was strong enough to handle these killers. They got the fates they deserved. They will spend the rest of their spiteful lives watching the American Spirit flourish outside their barred cell windows. They will die in prison.

In my father's time, when that flag went up on Iwo Jima, we triumphed abroad militarily, which was necessary and impressive. But after we won the war, the world was amazed that America emerged from history's darkest days with our democracy enhanced. The faces of the world's peoples turned like sunflowers to bask in the warm glow of American freedom and fairness. Russia, Japan and Germany are just three of the many countries that have gone democratic since the end of WWII. This unprecedented compliment of so many countries paying us the compliment of copying our democracy will surely go down in the history books as one of America's sterling accomplishments.

Military might does not guarantee freedom. If that were so, Hitler's and Tojo's societies would have been paradises.

The key is the American Spirit of fairness. How we treat each other according to the law. The law we agree is fair for all. The law we write down in books for our sons and daughters to obey.

Many Americans were traumatized by September 11, 2001. Iwo Jima traumatized my father. He never spoke about it. The worst battle in Marine Corps history was too horrible to verbalize, too painful for him. He lived a life in which actions spoke louder than words. After my dad died I spent five years researching his past. I studied the actions of my father over his lifetime, his examples, searching for the lessons.

I discovered that my young dad—at the age of 22—was among those who wrested wretched Mount Suribachi from Japan's finest and raised a flag on its crest. The Japanese slaughtered 84 percent of my dad's Iwo Jima buddies in the course of the battle. These were my dad's friends, guys he lived with, chummed with, for a year. Killed before his eyes. Later my mother told me my father cried in his sleep for four years after Iwo Jima.

With tears in their eyes and rifles in their hands, American boys on Iwo Jima took terrified "Japs" prisoner at gunpoint. And treated them according to rules. Rules based upon laws American society had agreed were fair. The American Spirit flourished amidst horrific slaughter on Iwo Jima. Today many term my father's generation as "greatest."

It was a generation that silenced our enemies while staying true to the Spirit of America.

We can do it again.

— **James Bradley**, author of
Flyboys and *Flags of Our Fathers*

The Fourth of July was always a hot morning with the smell of new mown grass in the air and hydrangea and rhododendron blooming at the edge of the woods. My father led our family parade with his head wrapped in a bloody bandage made with a torn sheet and some tomato sauce. My brother Ben carried one of my mother's hatboxes and played it like a kettledrum. The rest of us marched along, tunelessly tootling "Yankee Doodle Dandy" on school recorders or shouldering broomstick muskets, followed by the family dog. Suburban patriots, we went up and down the driveway past the glorious flag hung from an upstairs window to honor the brave militia which had won our country's freedom almost 200 years earlier. I didn't know what freedom was, but I had my marching orders.

As a teenager I was taken to Lexington and Concord, Mass., to see the bridge where American liberty began when "the embattled farmers stood, /And fired the shot heard round the world," as Ralph Waldo Emerson put it in 1836. The Concord River flowed gently between green banks under a simple footbridge; it was hard to imagine a war there. I didn't know what war was; I didn't know what freedom was. I had no dreams of raising a family, or becoming a writer, or any of the things to which freedom is as necessary as air is to breathe.

Last night I walked down to the embankment above the East River with my son to watch the fireworks. We stood looking downriver toward the fireworks barges anchored against the tide where the British once landed at Kips Bay. Here in Manhattan, crowds of people lined the riverfront and I heard French and Italian spoken and even British accents. Policemen checked bags and stopped pedestrians at the entrance to the footbridge over the F.D.R. Drive. When I asked why the drive wasn't opened the way it had been last year, one of the policemen said, "These are different circumstances."

People don't talk about September 11 all the time anymore; they don't have to. Living here in the bull's-eye of the terrorists' target we all have it in the back of our minds all the time: the dreadful losses, the awful possibilities, the fear that is not quite enough to drive us to a safer place if there is a safer place. In the days before *this* Fourth of July, every time firecrackers went off, dozens of people called the police.

Memory is mysterious. Images of our carefree Independence Day parade are now overlaid with images of people falling from windows with flames behind them and our wounded, smoldering skyline, and blocks of my city covered in ashes. My father died 20 years ago this summer. I remember a widow I met at Ground Zero who told me her husband used to go 100 floors for a cigarette break—and how much she prayed that day that he had broken his vow not to smoke at work.

Over the river last night there were explosions of golden light and glowing, falling rockets and breathtaking flowers of red and blue blossoming in the night sky. We stood in a little park on 52nd Street where people have planted abundant gardens. We were crowded together, but no one took the liberty of stepping over the railing into the garden in order to get a better view. When the fireworks turned the river red with their glow and then green and then gold, we clapped and hollered and cheered. I cheered for the joy of being with my son, the joy of living in a place where I can vote and have it matter, where I can write without fear, and where I can raise my children in a way that promises them freedom. Now that I know what freedom is.

— **Susan Cheever**, author of *As Good As I Could Be* and *Home Before Dark*

New Orleans, 9 a.m. It is already 90 hot and soupy degrees out there. I poke my head out on the balcony under the magnolia and retreat back into the humming comfort of my AC–cooled bed. Laura is brewing tea in the kitchen. I turn on CNN. Dear Lord, I say, please don't make this Fourth of July too memorable. This is my second favorite holiday, almost as good as Thanksgiving. There is no gift-giving, no religious significance. Families burn meat together to celebrate the independence of the Republic. There is none of the sentimentality and guilt of Mother's Day. I remember certain past Fourths: watching the fireworks at the Inner Harbor in Baltimore with visitors from abroad; lying on a hill in Boulder, Colo., eating fried chicken and potato salad with (nonvegetarian) Buddhists and poets; floating in the ocean in Hawaii watching the faint reddish flares of a distant fireworks display; trying to go to the American Embassy party in Prague, but getting distracted by a rowdy group of expats who celebrated by singing folk songs and passing around a bottle of wine under the Charles Bridge.

The Lord hears me. Nothing is happening on CNN. The Republic has nothing more to fear than corporate crooks.

10 a.m. After trying in vain to lure Laura back into bed ("It's the Fourth, honey, let's set off the fireworks") I get up, dress, and go to the corner store for a gallon of water and a newspaper. There are festive signs. The hot-dog cart is already out of the garage on the next block, sporting a passel of flags. A street guy has propped up one of his artworks in the store.

It's a drawing of Laffite's Tavern on Bourbon Street: little blue figures run all over the edges. "Blue dogs," he explains, "they are taking over everything." He hands me a Xerox copy and asks for "whatever you can afford." I give him two dollars. The blue dogs are a New Orleans thing. The guy is right. They have taken over. It's hard to explain. You have to be here.

12 noon. I've magneted the Laffite-Tavern-with-dogs drawing on the refrigerator. We go out. An Uncle Sam swigging a beer goes by. He's one of my neighbors, but I barely recognize him under his white beard. Uncle Sam is probably going to be in The Parade of Heroes, which will pass by the window of my favorite bar, Molly's at the Market, on Decatur Street, at more-or-less 3 p.m. Time is approximate in this town. Drinking a beer at noon is for adjusting the clock.

12:30 p.m. We go for lunch in a new diner that sits where three restaurants failed in one year. This one looks like it might make it. It's clean, the menu is spare, and the help is cute. A man eating eggs Benedict greets me. "I just read your last book," he says with a Latin accent. "Loved it." I remember him: He is a chef, member of the "4-N Boyz," who meet regularly to eat and watch soccer. They take turns doing the cooking. He is joined at his table by a guy who looks dressed by the Russian Mafia; Cartier watch, Bond Street suit. I am already broiling in my T-shirt, but this guy is crisp as iceberg lettuce. I raise my fist: "Viva Brazilian soccer! What a win!" They both raise their fists back.

3 p.m. Laura and I grab two stools at the window at Molly's, order a couple of patriotic martinis, and get ready for the parade. People line both sides of the street, waiting to be amused and ready to catch beads and trinkets.

There is a parade in New Orleans every other day, for any reason whatsoever, so this isn't so unusual. Except for the timing, of course: the first Fourth since 9/11. After the police cars, ambulances, and fire engines go screeching by, a huge Liberty Bell made out of foam appears, escorted by some Revolutionary War soldiers throwing beads to the crowd. The Bell is followed in short order by huge plaster heads of Lincoln and Andrew Jackson, a Statue of Liberty surrounded by Army nurses, three surplus amphibious vehicles, an enormous eagle with orange claws draped in a starry flag, and, finally, a genuine New Orleans brass band without which no parade is complete. A troop of horseback freedom riders brings up the rear. The parade is somewhat disappointing by local standards, but this is Harrah's Casino Parade of Heroes. Harrah's has been doing a lot of public relations in the city, and this parade seems more like a procession of losers forced into service by the casino in exchange for an extension of credit. No matter, it is quite amusing, especially after the second martini.

5 p.m. Across the street at Margaritaville, some musician friends are getting set to play, so we surrender our front row seats at Molly's and amble over. The blues trio is hot and the tourists, loaded down with beads, are having a good time. We have some well-done cheeseburgers and then it hits me: the

feeling. It is the Fourth, in New Orleans, with great music and friendly folks. Things are normal. So far. Our table gets crowded as more and more people show up. Somebody eats half my French fries.

9 p.m. A merry party of us heads to the riverfront for the fireworks. It is an abbreviated show, nothing extravagant by our impossibly high standards, but it is perfect. My mantra is: nothing too extraordinary. Please. A kind of hushed modesty prevails in the crowd.

10:30 p.m. After the fireworks, we go to another jazz joint, The Spotted Cat, where more of our bohemian pals have gathered to celebrate the pleasure of being alive in New Orleans, U.S.A., in the 21st century.

Midnight: the band does a funky version of "America the Beautiful." The Fourth is over, we are feeling fine. Life is good, let's hope it stays that way. Easy, CNN.

— **Andrei Codrescu**, author of *Casanova in Bohemia*

London on the Fourth of July was gray, damp, cold, and unremarkable. A month earlier, England had been a riot of patriotic colors as it celebrated the Queen's 50-Year Jubilee; and even two weeks before, flags and nationalistic T-shirts were everywhere as the English cheered on their World Cup team. By early July, however, the normal English reticence about patriotism had reasserted itself, and so it seemed inappropriate for American visitors to make much of the Fourth. A few London pubs had hung large American flags above their doors, hoping to attract American students to come in and celebrate. But about the only other public notice July 4 attracted was a series of excoriating articles in the British press about American foreign policy. (AMERICA: ROGUE NATION, the *Daily Mirror* announced on its front page.)

In America, many things have seemed profoundly different since September 11, and the lives of some Americans have still not returned to what once seemed normal. There have been too many warnings of imminent attacks; too many doomsday scenarios splashed across the front pages; too many politicians trying to exploit our fears. In New York, there have been too many physical reminders of a uniquely terrible moment in our history. But to the English, and to much of the rest of the world, the shock of September 11 wore off long ago, and our continued preoccupation with it seems to some people a sign of excessive self-regard. "A dreadful business, September 11," a friend—a formidable older English woman—said to us that week. "We all prayed for you. But you just have to carry on, don't you?" The English, of course, have prided themselves for decades on their ability to carry on—through the blitz and through the many years of IRA terrorism all over the country. We Americans used to pride ourselves on being immune from such things, and we have had difficulty confronting our lost sense of invulnerability.

And yet we do, on the whole, carry on pretty well after all. Most people continue to work and play more or less as usual, to care for their families, to plan for the future. They confine their fears to small corners of their minds and move on with their lives. Most Americans I know celebrated the Fourth of July pretty much as they always have, despite the drumbeat of warnings of terrorist attacks that did not come. Our parades and picnics and fireworks and funny hats, our oversize flags on view everywhere, our sentimental patriotism may all seem silly and self-indulgent to our friends abroad. But I missed them this year—not because they would have helped me cope with the post–September 11 world, but because they would have reassured me that the pre–September 11 America is still very much alive.

— **Alan Brinkley**, author of *The Unfinished Nation* and *Liberalism and Its Discontents*

Long's Peak, Rocky Mountain National Park, Colo./Beth Wald/Aurora

To spend July Fourth in another country is to realize that you are more American than you ever imagined. To spend this July Fourth at a conference where hundreds of people from around the world are gathered to talk about the uses of humor and comedy is to be reassured about the possibility that the best in us will have the strength to override the worst in us. It is to recognize the spiritual generosity of most, the intellectual exuberance of some, and the desire—on the part of all—to see laughter and life triumph over dogma and death.

It is also to realize, while hearing "Born in the U.S.A." played by a one-man Italian band during a gala dinner held on the battlements of a medieval castle—in the background, scholars from Israel, Egypt and the Netherlands discussing the fundamental importance of the knock-knock joke—that life can still be very, very funny.

I am spending the Fourth of July neither at a potluck picnic in Connecticut where I teach nor at a backyard barbecue in Brooklyn where so many of my relatives are at this moment, but in Italy—the country that my paternal grandparents left in order to "Make America." I am presenting a scholarly paper at the aforementioned conference on humor. No kidding. I wrote much of my presentation, as I am writing this essay, on a computer located inside a medieval fortress (the absurdity of this does not escape me). If you had told my Sicilian grandmother that her youngest granddaughter would return to Italy as an academic, she would have laughed for five full minutes, pausing only to catch her breath and wipe her eyes with the hem of her apron. *Professoressa* is what they call me here, and I can only imagine that word being addressed to me in a tone of affectionate but unmistakable contempt by any member of my family, making it sound like *La Principessa,* which is what they used to call me if I refused to eat all the gnocchi.

But I enjoy the luxury of being teased by my family about my "academic work"—a phrase they consider a contradiction in terms—because I realize that I was able to achieve the academy in no small measure because my grandmother, like so many other immigrants, had the courage and determination to make a better life. At 17, she left behind everything she ever knew in order to begin again in an unknown place, the address of a cousin sewn into her pocket. What she left behind in her native village was remorseless, enforced poverty and ignorance, true, but also astonishing beauty, history and the warm sun of the only world she had ever known. She took a leap. She met my grandfather on Houston Street in New York City and together they raised a family that in no way replicated the ones they had left. Their children had choices—not many, but some—and that was what my grandparents wanted for them. From humble ingredients they prepared feasts, and in many ways the children were the guests at this table. If we learned that we had to sing for our supper by working harder and succeeding sooner than many of our peers, well, "too bad." That was the deal. And it was more than fair.

If it did not take the family very many generations to produce a *professoressa,* that might be because things move fast in America. A hundred years is a long time for us, just as a hundred miles is a long way over here in Italy. Time moves fast when good things are happening.

Which leads to the reflection, on this strange Fourth of July, that time moves almost not at all after a tragedy occurs. Is this why September 11 is still with us every day?

I sit in this castle and am afraid of the quite natural impulse our nation has felt to close the doors and draw up the bridges, making a fortress of our own in order to keep ourselves safe. To be walled up is not to be safe; it is to be stagnant, paralyzed, suffocated—and without options, without freedom. We cannot risk re-creating in our own country those barriers and boundaries that our ancestors had to leap over or crawl under in order to "Make America" in the first place.

With our pain and pride, we feel an urge to threaten the world with a closed fist rather than offer the world an open hand or the possibility of an embrace. I hope we resist this urge. Battles and brawls create changed situations, but these can be altered anew by the next battle or brawl. Community is more permanent.

Community has a sound. It sounds light and airy, like freedom. You can hear laughter. People are saying over here, at this humor conference, that it's nice to hear America laughing again, albeit more uneasily than it might have laughed on September 8, 9 or 10 of 2001. The return of laughter, they are saying, is undoubtedly a good sign.

I agree. Maybe the fist will loosen a bit. Maybe barriers will come down or will never be built. That would be good for Americans at home and good for America in the world.

Please understand, I am not suggesting that world peace will be achieved by a cross-cultural understanding of the knock-knock joke. What I am saying is: To laugh with another person is to share, for a glittering moment, a perspective and an intimacy. Worth exporting? Hey, it couldn't hurt.

— **Regina Barreca**, editor of *Don't Tell Mama: The Penguin Book of Italian American Writing*

P hotographed from the air—not that this could have happened on July 4, all air traffic near downtown Chicago had been rerouted, just as a precaution . . .

Photographed from the air, the scene along Chicago's lakefront might have appeared pretty much as it would on any previous Independence Day. The joggers along the edge of Lake Michigan, the families having picnics on the grass, the choose-up-sides teams playing soccer in the park, the young men and women flirting in the sand on Oak Street Beach, the bicyclists and soda-pop vendors and Frisbee flippers and swimmers, the lifeguards poised near the water . . .

Photographed from the air, captured in a panoramic shot on a glossy postcard, all would have appeared just fine—the Fourth of July, any year at all.

Yet this was not any year at all, and the differences—small, silent differences, differences we all still are trying to figure out—were not of the sort that can be viewed in any photograph, whether it was taken from a distance or from just a few feet away.

There is a wariness still with us—on July 4 and every other day—that is at the same time manifestly understandable and mutedly subduing. Ever since September, we as a nation have been checking off every first-since holiday—first Thanksgiving since September 11, first Christmas, first New Year's Eve, first day of a new year, first Memorial Day—as if when the checklist has been completed, when we have gone all the way around the calendar, have completed the first lap . . .

Well . . . what?

It is as if we have been telling ourselves that once we make it back to September again, once every day of the year since last September has been lived, then things will be as they were. Then we will be back to being the people we were very early on that September Tuesday morning—the people we were before the first airplane approached a tower in Manhattan.

So, in ways no photograph will ever be able to discern, because even the finest photographs by the most brilliant photographers have their limits . . .

In ways invisible to the eye, but clearly evident to the human heart, we go about our business seeming to be pretty much the same as we were before, or at least pretty much healed. In Chicago on the Fourth of July, on the gorgeous, sun-washed shores of Lake Michigan, there was laughter and welcoming shouts and smoke rising from the many barbecue grills;

there were romances forming and romances ending and music from thousands upon thousands of radios and CD headsets. Boats zipped through the water, and babies looked trustingly up at their parents, and tossed-on-the-pavement newspaper pages told stories that were disturbing (American corporations swindling American citizens through accounting chicanery) and comforting (American baseball teams squaring off against each other in pennant races that, with the symmetry of their meticulous statistical measurement, gave the illusion of order and stability).

Yet of course we are not the same. There is a wariness, a constant little intake of breath—it's there even when we forget that it's there—that we could not have expected to have dissipated by July 4, and that we should not expect to have vanished by the time we pass the 11th day of September, a year after. The checking-off of days, no matter how well intentioned, cannot be catharsis; this is going to take far more than a year, this is a journey without a map, and we all do our best, knowing somewhere at our very core that the answer, the end, remains far away, over some horizon we cannot yet even glimpse.

The prayer—never said aloud—is that September 11, 2001, will forever remain the worst day. Because to think otherwise—to think that that September Tuesday might have been merely the prelude, might have been the overture, not the opera itself. . . To think about that is almost too much to bear. So on July 4—like any other day, but different than any other day—we celebrated our independence, our freedom, in millions of small ways, smiling for snapshots and letting the sun beat down on us, grinning at jokes and turning the volume up when a favorite song came on the air, watching the skies for clouds that might throw unwelcome shadows. The national portrait—taken from far enough away—might have been interchangeable with the portrait from any other Fourth of July. Some things you cannot see.

And where will we all be next July 4—how will our American portrait appear once we have made our way around the calendar one more time, step-by-step, day-and-night by day-and-night?

May there be abundant tranquillity next July 4, abundant joy. May the breath we constantly hold inside of us—that intake of breath we sometimes forget is even there—have been released, just a little bit. As we continue, together, to find our way home.

— **Bob Greene**, author of *Once Upon a Town: The Miracle of the North Platte Canteen* and *Duty: A Father, His Son, and the Man Who Won the War*

I hear America singing.
The Giants win the pennant. My country 'tis of thee.
Ask not what your country can do for you.
Paper or plastic? Early-bird special. Like a fish needs a
    bicycle.
I have a dream. Buy low, sell high.
One small step for mankind. Some fan has a lucky souvenir.
All your soft-rock favorites. Sitting in a tree, k-i-s-s-i-n-g.
Mountain Dew. See you in September. You're not going out
    looking like that.

Havlicek stole the ball. Rockets' red glare.
Rendezvous with destiny. Rock around the clock.
Strawberry shortcake, blueberry pancakes, cranberry
    cocktail, blackberry wine, huckleberry pie.
When in the course of human events. Never undersold.
National League, National Lampoon, National Association
of Manufacturers, national nightmare is over.
Wait till next year. Tear down this wall. Lake-effect
    snowstorm.
Tennessee Waltz, Texas two-step, the Virginia Reel.
Indiana University of Pennsylvania, Washington University
    in St. Louis.

The corn is as high as an elephant's eye.
Earned run average, Equal Rights Amendment.
Independence Avenue. Broadway Joe. Because that's where
    the money is.
NBA, NYPD, NAFTA, NAACP, NCAA, NYSE.
Hail to the victors valiant. Thanksgiving turkey with oyster
    stuffing.
Daniel Webster, Daniel Boone, Pat Boone, boondoggle,
    Doggie Julian.
Separation of powers. Trick or treat. Swimmers take your
    mark.
Bagels and brats, pirogi and pad thai, spumoni and
    souvlaki (extra feta please).
Fifty-seven varieties, 54–40 or fight, 56 consecutive games.
First and 10, five and dime.
From California to the New York island. From Burlington to
Block Island. From sea to shining sea. From Maine to
California. From here to there to everywhere.
The Weather Channel. The buck stops here.

Curt Flood, the Johnstown Flood, Muddy Waters, Love that
Dirty Water.
Poland Spring Water, spring training, training wheels,
Wheel of Fortune.
Dairy Queen, Queen for a Day, Queen City, city chicken,
chicken on the grill, grilled cheese.
First amendment, Second Manassas, third of a nation,
Fourth of July, fifth of Scotch, sixth man, seventh-inning
stretch,
⅛ (Eddie Gaedel's number),
Bottom of the ninth, 10th Mountain Division.
I have not yet begun to fight. There is such a thing as a man
being too proud to fight.
I will fight no more forever.
Bury my heart at Wounded Knee.

Boston baked beans, Buffalo wings, Cincinnati chili,
Chicago pizza.
Charleston Chew, Maine lobster, Memphis BBQ, Maryland
crab, Michigan cherries.
Florida stone crabs, Omaha Steaks, Vermont maple syrup,
Washington apples.
Southern fried chicken. With French fries.

Rhode Island clam chowder, Manhattan clam chowder,
New England clam chowder.
Newt Gingrich, Newton Minnow, Newton North High.
You're darned tootin', I like Fig Newton.

Winston-Salem, Wynton Marsalis, Marvelous Marvin, Dean
Martin, Ned Martin,
Ricky Martin, Ricky Ricardo, Lucille Ball, play ball.
CTA, FDR, MVP, DFW, MBA, PDA. All the way with LBJ.
The right to boo the Dodgers. Want to super-size that?
Who had the tuna salad? Rock 'n' roll is here to stay.
Moon River, Wally Moon, Wallace Cleaver, Cleveland
Browns, Willie Brown.
With malice toward none, with charity for all, with firmness
in the right
As God gives us to see the right, let us strive on to finish the
work we are in,
To bind up the nation's wounds, to care for him who shall
have borne
The battle and for his widow and his orphan.
Sweet land of liberty. Let's roll.
— **David M. Shribman**, Washington Bureau Chief,
The Boston Globe, and editor of *I Remember My Teacher*

The number of those massacred we have not exactly determined, as many remains of charred bodies are found in the ruins of burned buildings. We have been engaged ever since in burying the dead. I believe there have been over 120 houses burned. All the business part of the town is in ashes, except three stores.

— R.G. Elliott, Lawrence, Kans., resident
describing the aftermath of Quantrill's Raid, 1863

Prior to September 11, probably no American community, with the possible exception of Oklahoma City, had more brutal knowledge of terrorism than Lawrence, Kans. An eclectic college town of 80,000 located 30 minutes west of Kansas City, Lawrence evokes the neighborly decency of unlocked doors, white picket fences, and the sort of galloping normality that moves media types to speak glibly of The Heartland. The town sprang to life in the turbulent 1850s, when the Massachusetts legislature chartered the New England Emigrant Aid Society to help colonize Kansas' virgin prairies for the abolitionist cause. Morally driven New Englanders responded to the call—with a gun in one hand, sneered Stephen A. Douglas, and a Bible in the other.

The society invested $20,000 in the Free State Hotel, as symbolic of its culture, and therefore as vulnerable to attack by fanatics, as the Twin Towers were to latter-day terrorists confusing murder with martyrdom. On May 21, 1856, a raiding party of pro-slavery Missourians briefly planted a "Southern Rights" flag atop the hotel before torching the place and ransacking the editorial offices of the nearby *Herald of Freedom*. Undaunted, free state legislators reconvened at Topeka on July 4, only to be dispersed at gunpoint by federal troops answering to President Franklin Pierce, a blundering mediocrity whose feeble statesmanship earned him history's scorn as a doughface—a northern man with southern principles.

Thus did Bleeding Kansas foreshadow fraternal war on a continental scale. Shortly after daybreak on August 21, 1863, a 26-year-old former schoolteacher and accused horse thief named William C. Quantrill led 450 pro-slavery guerillas in a savage raid on Lawrence. The town awoke to shouts of "On to the hotel!" as Quantrill's men, Frank and Jesse James among them, swept down Massachusetts Street to plunder the Eldridge House, successor to the gutted Free State Hotel. In the ensuing butchery, the cruelest blows were directed against African

Americans who had made Lawrence an important way station on the Underground Railroad. One black preacher was shot in his doorway as his daughter looked on. An ancient runaway slave survived the first fusillade by playing dead. Somehow he managed to rise to his feet and hobble towards safety, until stragglers in Quantrill's ranks, mindful of their orders to kill every man old enough to carry a gun, finished him off.

After four hours of slaughter, Quantrill's army retreated south. It left Lawrence in flames and nearly 200 corpses to mark one of the worst massacres of American civilians before September 11. One hundred thirty-nine years later, tourists come to read bronze plaques along thriving Massachusetts Street. The casual visitor might be forgiven for thinking that in Lawrence, time is measured BQ (Before Quantrill) and AQ (After Quantrill). A rebuilt Eldridge House rubs shoulders with the Free State Brewery and a movie theater called Liberty Hall. Besides Civil War buffs, the town attracts literary pilgrims following in the footsteps of Langston Hughes and William S. Burroughs. To basketball fans, Lawrence is best known as the home of Dr. James Naismith, the game's inventor, and the only coach in University of Kansas history to suffer a losing record.

Perched atop Mount Oread, once occupied by Quantrill-posted lookouts, KU welcomed news at the start of its 2001–2002 school year that it had been ranked among the nation's top 50 public universities by *U.S. News & World Report*. On September 10 ground was broken for a pioneering brain-imaging center. The next morning 39 students, faculty and staff members were scheduled to fly to the nation's capital for a seminar on the federal government. They never went. Instead, Quantrill's ghost stalked Mount Oread, as a new generation of terrorists pursued the medieval contradiction of holy war.

As news of the atrocities in New York and Washington filtered across campus, student body president Justin Mills declared his intention to camp out for 48 hours, or until he raised $25,000—roughly one dollar for every student—to assist victims and their families. Over $30,000 flooded in. Still more would be collected for a September 11 scholarship fund cochaired by Bill Clinton and Bob Dole—the same Dole who had left KU six decades earlier to avenge the attack on Pearl Harbor. Now—today—nearly 10 months after September 11, the white ribbons have been taken down, but KU's ubiquitous Jayhawk still shares window space with the American eagle along Massachusetts Street. On June 30, getting a jump on Independence Day celebrations, worshipers at Plymouth Congregational Church, whose 19th century predecessor fell victim to Quantrill's torches, listened to Reverend Peter Luckey preach on "The Work of Freedom." *In freedom's house there are many mansions.* Hardly had Rev. Luckey stepped down from his pulpit than disciples of a different sort commandeered the intersection of Massachusetts and 11th Streets. In their hands they held signs directing passing motorists to HONK FOR HEMP. Elsewhere on Massachusetts Street, the Leonard Peltier Defense Committee would spend July sifting 30,000 pages of FBI documents freshly obtained through the Freedom of Information Act. The committee remained unwavering in its support of the Native American activist jailed following the 1975 slaying of two FBI agents on South Dakota's Pine Ridge Indian Reservation. One of the handful of American communities founded to advance a political agenda, Lawrence has not lost its taste for unpopular causes.

Nor does the town lack for homegrown controversies. For three days each year, within precisely set if loosely enforced hours, it is possible for Independence Day revelers to use Saturn Missiles and Festival Balls and hissing "worms" that creep colorfully across sunbaked pavements. Because Lawrence prohibits the sale of fireworks within city limits, entrepreneurs with an eye for fine print take over parking lots on the outskirts of town for several days before the holiday. From here they do a robust trade in sparklers and exploding shells. If anything, business may be too good: Last year an apartment house caught fire, and Lawrence police responded to 260 fireworks-related calls during the first week of July.

Vendors anticipate a spike in sales this year, mirroring the surge of patriotic feelings since September 11. Whether in recognition of the national mood, or in hope of shifting the focus away from backyard celebrations marred by illegal pipe rockets and homemade explosives, city commissioners have added $4,000 to the usual budget of $8,000 for the Jaycees' big fireworks show on the banks of the Kansas River. It's the closest thing in town to an official celebration. Like the Republic whose birthday it commemorates, the Fourth in Lawrence is decentralized. Far removed from the bomb-sniffing dogs and patrol jets of urban America, the observance makes up in spontaneous emotion what it lacks in spread-eagle oratory or sanctioned Sousa. Especially this year.

Consider the Morgans of Inverness Drive. If communities have pillars, then Scott Morgan and his wife Kathleen surely qualify. After several years on the local school board, Scott recently graduated to the title of president. Under the most favorable circumstances, this is an act of selflessness. In a time of budgetary cuts and teacher layoffs, anyone brave enough to take the job can expect vigorous abuse in place of the customary indifference. Scott comes by his sense of obligation naturally. The son of a legendary political correspondent for *The*

Kansas City Star, he received an early indoctrination in backyard patriotism. When the village fathers of Shawnee banned fireworks on the Fourth, Ray Morgan wangled the only exemption in town. It died with Ray.

Hoping that history won't repeat itself in Lawrence, Scott has urged city commissioners to think twice before carrying out their threat to cancel fireworks sales. In the meantime, he is passing on to his three children the traditions of a flag-waving childhood. Each July 3 the Morgans invite dozens of neighbors and friends to assemble with their casserole dishes and Uncle Sam hats for a driveway party. "It's not terribly organized," Kathleen says of the event. "We just eat a lot and blow stuff up." This sets the tone for a holiday whose very artlessness testifies to its sincerity. On the morning of the Fourth impromptu parades snake their way through several Lawrence neighborhoods. Fire trucks lead children on bicycles and young mothers pushing strollers festooned in patriotic colors. At the Budde residence on Wildwood Drive, a ceremonial flag-raising precedes the reading of the Declaration of Independence

by U.S. Circuit Court Judge Deanell Tacha.

That the nation's birthday should also witness the simultaneous deaths of Thomas Jefferson and John Adams, precisely 50 years after they served as midwives to the Republic, lends an eerie, providential resonance to Independence Day. Far less notice is paid to the only American President born on July 4. Over the years Calvin Coolidge has been represented as a deservedly modest figure—what H. L. Mencken called "the greatest man ever to come out of Plymouth Notch, Vermont." Yet if the Founders' legacy is representative government—a faith that makes heroes out of stockbrokers and firefighters—then democracy's future rests more with the Coolidges than with the demigods of Philadelphia. Besides, grandiosity is as alien to Kansas as the pelican.

In this time of Enrons and WorldComs, Coolidge's remarks of July 4, 1926, have never been more topical: "We live in an age of science and of abounding accumulation of material things. These did not create our Declaration. Our Declaration created them. The things of the spirit come first. Unless we cling to that, all our material prosperity, overwhelming though it may appear, will turn to a barren scepter in our grasp." As understated as Coolidge's passion, the rituals of Lawrence's Fourth give proof of the strength of post–September 11 institutions. What more could one expect of a community whose motto is From Ashes to Immortality. The best way to preserve our freedoms, the town suggests, is to practice them. That includes a quiet defiance of those who would betray liberty by imposing conformity. As night falls, little else in Lawrence is quiet. The near-constant sound of exploding shells suggests small arms fire. Close your eyes and it becomes possible to imagine, amid the acrid smoke clouds rising from the town below, what terrorism might have sounded like in August 1863.

The image of freedom under attack is quickly superseded by a still greater explosion, as a pair of B-1 bombers based at McConnell Air Force Base outside Wichita make their annual traverse of eastern Kansas. On Inverness Drive, the Morgan children are reciting the Declaration of Independence, like their father and grandfather before them. The next morning the slopes of Oread will be littered with the spent shells of Dancing Butterflies, Golden Silverflower and Colored Aviation Lamps. Fresh ammunition, so to speak, for a debate as old as America's attempt to square the circle of ordered liberty.

— **Richard Norton Smith**, author of *Patriarch: George Washington and the New American Nation*

We sat on top of quilts and sleeping bags and picnic debris on the crowded lawn of the Old Courthouse in Decatur, Ga., waiting for twilight and fireworks. In the old-time bandstand, a brass band played Sousa. As the sky darkened, my small son—who was under the impression that we were camping there and who had zipped himself inside a sleeping bag in the 90-degree heat and then requested a pillow—asked in his high-pitched voice, loud enough for everyone to hear: "Mommy, how old is the earth?" The responsive laughter all around us told me that everyone was familiar with this classic question on a first night spent under the stars, and that no one sitting nearby knew the correct answer either. One stranger called out: "I'm a preschool teacher. Just say, 'How old do you think the earth is, dear?'"

Crammed all together, our beach chairs rubbing up against each other's, the scent of mosquito-repellent mingling with the bouquet of the uncorked bottles of wine, a casual conversational tone was struck. Beside us sat an immigrant from Turkey, a young man of 25 who'd come to his first Fourth of July picnic as the guest of his English teacher's family. On the other side, a middle-aged, heavyset blonde woman unfolded her lawn chair. Of an old Atlanta family, and with the drawl to prove it, she mentioned she was waiting for her guest, her foster son, one of the Lost Boys of the Sudan.

In short: an American scene.

When the ear-popping noise started, were the colors overhead brighter than the colors of our upturned faces? Within the hectare of dry grass, paper plates, and empty Coke cans, the cheeks of African, European, Latino, Middle-Easterner and Asian sparkled in reflected light.

The world is a smaller place since 9/11. Now that death and destruction have been visited upon our own cities, the bombings in other cities shake us. We are not immune to the world's sorrow; we cannot wall ourselves off from it, nor should we. I agree daily with my neighbor's bumper sticker: IF YOU WANT PEACE, WORK FOR JUSTICE.

The fireworks in the skies all over America are the expressions of joy of a citizenry unused to cowering from attacks. In America, only small children jump in fright at the sounds of explosion. The war waged in 1776, the bullets that flew, the cannon that fired, have evolved over two centuries into these artful arcs of color. This is what we now understand by "the rockets' red glare."

The immigrants who crept in among us on the muggy courthouse lawn on the Fourth of July marveled less, I suspect, at the colors thrown against the dark sky than at the relaxed motley holiday crowd of us who enjoyed them.

"Can fireworks kill you if they fall on you?" asked my son from the sweaty, muffled innards of his sleeping bag.

"No," we said, being certain of our answer this time.

— **Melissa Fay Greene**, author
of *Praying for Sheetrock*

It was early morning of July 4, 2002—around 5:30, I think. My wife, our three sons and their families, plus my sister and her husband, 18 in all, were still asleep in our camp on an island on New Hampshire's Lake Winnepesaukee. The lake was calm, like a mirror, the sky clear. It would, I decided, be a gorgeous day just like when I was in New York City almost 10 months earlier. The image of those huge trailer trucks loaded with medical supplies barreling down Fifth Avenue, accompanied by police on motorcycles, heading toward all that billowing smoke, flashed through my mind. It often does.

I settled myself onto the bench I built there by the water years ago and sipped my coffee. The sun glistened through the tall pines behind me. From afar I heard the sound of an outboard motor but the huge lake before me, in its myriad undulating reflections, seemed to be otherwise free of human activity. Then, far down near The Witches and Forty Islands, I saw a dark, faintly ominous-looking band of ruffled water creeping slowly toward me along the entire breadth of the lake from Meredith Bay to Moultonborough Neck. Mysteriously, there were long-ago voices and laughter like distant music. Although it was already warm, I felt goosebumps. Would my family, I wondered, be able to persevere through what lay ahead for all of us Americans? Would we be brave enough? Would I?

A solitary leaf on the poplar tree leaning over the shore near me began to flap lazily as if in preparation for the daily summertime wind—inevitably on its way as always. While I waited for it in the temporary magical stillness of early morning, just as I have done a thousand times before, I looked across the water to the hills that rise over the faraway shores and then on and on beyond for miles and miles of those misty-blue mountains to the north.

— **Judson D. Hale Sr.**, Editor in Chief, *Yankee* magazine and *The Old Farmer's Almanac*

Just as Thanksgiving is for families, as Presidents' Day is for shoppers and Valentine's is for sweethearts, the Fourth of July is for crowds. It is almost your patriotic duty to get out there and sweat with everybody else—a picnic at least, but better yet, on the beach, or in a stadium, or at a concert or pressed together wherever, watching fireworks. We join, proudly, with our countrypeople. The numbers hearten us and encourage, nationally, both love and bravado.

On this first Fourth of July after September 11, I, however, found myself all but alone. I only ventured out once, to a deserted drugstore. Maybe that is good. Certainly it is for reflection. So, here I was, at home, reflecting, under the same kind of perfect cloudless, baby-blue sky that the bats of hell suddenly flew out of 10 months ago.

I still find that it is difficult for us to believe that such a thing actually happened to us. Equally so, even now we yet find it hard to fathom why anyone would wish to harm us so willfully. Especially for a nation, famously, of immigrants, we are not very good at looking back in at ourself. But then, apart from taking in people, we are much better at export. That's what we do. America sends stuff out. Ideas, attitudes, customs, styles. That's why we were the only people in the whole world this summer who didn't care jack about the World Cup of soccer. That's somebody else's thing, and never mind that it is everybody else's thing. Boy, does that drive the rest of humankind nuts. We talk about un-American. Well, we are so often un-world. And hooray for our team.

But it's in that same fashion, I suppose, why we also feel that it's just not necessary for us to go along and sign international treaties—concerning everything from land mines to global warming. Independence Day? We don't need a Day to remind the rest of the world what an independent bunch of cusses we are. In this advanced stage of globalization we can't any longer be (that old-world word) isolationist, but we are still, really, quite, well: independent.

So it seemed especially unreal that we, over here, were attacked. We were terror-fied. We were wounded. Then we got mad. We still are. And we have every right, in response, to be belligerent, even bellicose in the name of our sacred honor and our dear defense. Praise the Lord and pass the ammunition. Absolutely. Especially since: It was not our fault, not even a teensy-weensy bit. Still, I think that in the daily course of human events, a little American humility could also help us to win this war, this century.

I know this will get the Correct Police after me (if not at least Fox News), but I'm a little tired of us asking God to bless America. Look: God has already blessed America, more than anyone else. God has given us the most incredible natural bounty, and then escorted human beings from everywhere else—from England and Ireland, from Italy, from Africa, from the Philippines, from every nook and cranny on the globe—and brought them here to nourish the land and strengthen one another. Lord, but God has already done more than enough for America, blessings-wise.

Instead, in counterpoint to our vigilance and power, let us bless the world we rule with our generosity and understanding as much as with our majesty.

— **Frank Deford**, author of *An American Summer*

My husband, three-year-old son and I decided to spend the Fourth of July in Washington, D.C., this year not because we wanted to escape New York, where we live (although we know a few people who felt that way), or to spend the most patriotic of days in the most patriotic of places. It was simply that we were invited to a wedding and said, yes, we'd come.

The wedding wasn't until July 6, leaving the Fourth open. After a barbecue with friends, we raced down Connecticut Avenue to watch the fireworks from the bottom of the hill. We were too far away to hear the booms, which usually scare my son, but we could see the colors, bright and sparkly in the night sky. As I watched our little boy craning his neck, mesmerized, I said to my husband, "This is the first July Fourth he hasn't been afraid." This year of all years, when almost everyone is afraid of something, he didn't cry a bit.

This isn't the first time in the past year that my son has been my inspiration. He was only two and a half on September 11, too young to comprehend the destruction and death. He saw only a tiny bit of television that day, but it was enough to make him get out his toy fire trucks and announce that he was going to be a firefighter when he grew up, so that he could help people. As the rest of us wondered what to make of what had happened, his response was simple and direct: What could he do for someone else?

That was at home. At work, our readers' kids started sending us drawings of what they were feeling: drawings of planes

crashing and buildings burning and flags, lots and lots of flags. They wrote notes of thanks to the rescue workers and messages of sympathy to the children whose parents had died. It became my therapy to sort through their hundreds of drawings to decide which ones to publish in the magazine and which to send on to the relief organizations. The words and pictures of those thoughtful, generous children broke my heart and lifted my spirits.

On July 5 we had lunch at the home of some dear friends. Among the guests were a couple and their four-year-old son: three people who know something about tragedy. The fourth member of their family, a darling four-month-old girl, had died of a rare blood disorder nearly 10 months earlier, on September 14. In the same hours that the country was reeling from a terrorist attack, these parents had faced their own indescribable burden of taking their sick baby from the hospital so she could die peacefully at home, in their arms. And here they were now, sitting on the floor playing trucks and trains and Candyland, obviously enjoying their son, generous enough to dote

on ours. These are changed people, certainly, and I suspect there is a hole in their hearts that will never heal, but they go on living and loving and inspiring the rest of us with their strength and courage and determination to create a happy life for their son.

Life is hard, unspeakably hard, sometimes, and harder, surely, for some than for others. The wonder of it all, though, is how much good can spring from the bad. Somewhere, from deep within, amid impossible pain, comes the urge to give and to help and to recover. The worst sometimes inspires the best.

My friends' son has probably been their saving grace during these last 10 months, as, in a different way, my own sweet boy and all those readers' kids have been mine. Children have the noblest intentions—what can I do for someone else?—and their innocence reminds us to have good intentions too. They show us what is right and true in life. If they can do all that for us, surely the least we can do is draw on their inspiration to become our very best selves.

— **Andrea Barbalich**, Executive Editor, *Child* magazine

Juneau, Alaska/Brian Wallace

Typical Independence Day in the Northwest: The parade was rained on, the yard work surrendered to the squall. I did not even partake of the hot dog or the hamburger. But I did eat an ear of corn.

The corn was presented to me hot off the grill, sheathed tightly in its suit of leaves. The tassel hung forth in a wilted curl, a few wisps charred to black. But when I peeled the scorched casing I found the kernels plump the whole way to the tip. No shrunken nibs where the fruiting body peters out— this whole ear was as juicy as a melon. A white ear whose cooking had given it an ashy cast. It was perhaps the best corn I'd ever tasted even though it looked so strange.

Of course there's corn and then there's corn: I mean the ear at the table, the individual ear, versus the crop that stretches across whole states. Zoom out from the cob and you get to Kansas. Zoom in and you get the kernels, lined up each by each.

July Fourth is rife with these perspective shifts as we zoom between individual rituals (eating corn) and collective ones (fireworks at the park). These collective rituals have the power to align us like light waves passing through a lens. Our necks crane to the sky in unison. Our oohs rise up as one. This year even the corniest (ha ha) civic rites assumed a different sort of gravity. The oompah band started playing down at the band-

stand, and we were compelled to hark.

But we were also called to private ceremonies, say, that of a man and a woman sharing a glass of wine on their back deck. The man is using the yard's tiki torches as a launch point for the Mad Dog Roman Candles he has bought from the school's fund-raiser fireworks stand. This is my husband, who has set an old asbestos shingle in the yard, where he ignites the Jack in the Box Surprises and the Peach Flower in Spring. Ordinarily I am afraid of fire during this three-day open season that our town allows for fireworks. But today I figure the rain will save us. The sparks sizzle in the wet lawn like grease.

From the back deck I also get a view of town, its sodium lamps glowing a cantaloupe color. At 10 o'clock the horizon is a greenish tawny smear, the deep blue of the sky inching down to meet it. I hear booms when the display in the park starts up. But I can't see it through the trees. What I can see is the blazing of individual rites: bottle rockets everywhere. Starburst mortars and white wormy things that rise with zigzag trails. With our individual pyrotechnics we're creating a sort of collective ritual, though its only organizing principle is chaos.

Tonight someone will (inadvertently) set fire to his house despite the rain, but I won't learn this until I read the morning paper. For now, it's me and my loved one alone in the dark, sending flares into the sky. If I zoom out I can see how the whole town sputters, how we are part of something larger and wilder than ourselves. Or I can zoom in on the sparkler my husband hands me so I can try to write my name on the night with flames. But the letters vanish quicker than they can be created. By midnight we are all engulfed in a sulfurous smoky haze.

— **Lucia Perillo**, author of *The Body Mutinies*

When Teddy Roosevelt visited Chautauqua he pronounced it "typically American, in that it is typical of America at its best." A century later his judgment remains sound. This little village, on the shore of Chautauqua Lake in western New York state, sleeps all winter but awakes by the Fourth of July, when its summer residents return; they open their houses, plant the petunias, hang the flags and set about their summer jobs of uplifting and restoring and improving themselves with a summer of lectures and concerts and brisk morning swims. It's the kind of place families come back to, year after year, children forming friendships in the same sandboxes where their parents met a generation before. Summer here is a kind of performance art, not just because there is a resident opera and dance company, lots of painters planted in front of easels along the lake, but because Chautauqua is a place of perfection, never achieved but ever aspired to, where most every house has a porch that acts as both stage and front row seat. One travels the summer from porch to porch, reuniting with friends, comparing best books read over the winter, or lessons learned, a child's triumph or struggle, a marriage suddenly shaky, a new business launched. Most of the action occurs offstage, during the winter, but in the summer the players come together again and compare and update, and it all really gets started around the Fourth of July, when even people who can only slip away for a week know that this is the week they will see everyone they know.

And so this year of all years, it was bound to be different.

For my family—my husband and two little girls, my brother and his wife, my mother—this summer had already promised to be different because it started back in April. We all came to Chautauqua early, because my father wanted to die here, in the place he called home, with its high concentration of happy memory and discovery and solace. He died on an April Tuesday, on a spring summer day, and neighbors brought pies and prayers and we spent a week together, arriving as eight, returning home as seven, with a plot chosen in the cemetery across the road. So in June when we arrived back to open the house for the summer, it was a moment of welcome and loss, of stocking a refrigerator and emptying closets, carefully putting away his wedding ring, his glasses, giving away his summer clothes, and receiving from every neighbor a story, a memory, a kindness, a consolation.

But there was another piece missing, another change. Ordinarily those initial summer conversations are as distinct as each family's story. This summer there was one story; if it was not the first question it was the second, especially because Chautauqua attracts a large number of New Yorkers, and they all had a story to tell to their summer friends from safer towns. Where were you that day? How did you hear? Who did you know?

The September 11 conversations were strange on the dock on a lovely day, when flaming skyscrapers could not seem further away and yet the memories were hot again. It was clear this Fourth would feel different, since the country whose birthday we celebrate felt different, much like a child who is so different at seven than at six, only one year and yet so much older. The songs are the same, as are the colors and bunting, the traditional nursery school parade into the center of town, the big band concert on the town square. And yet when the community came together that night in the amphitheater, parents and children and grandchildren, the spirit of celebration was wrapped in a spirit of chastened gratitude and abiding sorrow. When the orchestra played the themes of each branch of the military service and the veterans were invited to stand, there arose throughout the vast, 6,000-seat wooden hall generations of warriors, the men—almost all were men—of World War II and Korea and Vietnam and Desert Storm and perhaps, home on leave, the war we now fight. "Grandpa Howard should be here," my daughter said, for she knew my father had once been a soldier too, and she saw in the proud, serious faces of men standing all around her an echo of his face, his life. When it was time to sing "America the Beautiful" and "God Bless America," people rose without being asked, in a slowly breaking wave, and sang words that are no longer automatic.

Teddy Roosevelt seemed more prescient than ever this summer, for the day was a parade of reminders as well about what makes the country sturdy and supple.

That day, as every day, there were morning worship services all over the Chautauqua grounds, Methodists and Lutherans and Catholics and Quakers and Jews all meeting sometimes together, sometimes separately to explore the foundations of their faiths. Nathan Baxter, the dean of the National Cathedral in Washington who led the nation's prayer service on September 14, led morning worship, a continuing exploration of good and evil and the journey we are on. The Islamic expert and author Karen Armstrong, Chautauqua's theologian in residence for the summer, hosts a series of lectures on understanding Islam, not just faith and politics but art and culture. Other lectures are devoted to understanding Africa, or celebrating great women poets, or developments in world trade, or the ethical challenges of the information age.

A place where every point of view is welcomed; where multiple faiths are practiced, serially and simultaneously; where curiosity, varsity sport and ignorance are seen less as challenges than as opportunities, is a place deserving celebration. To celebrate America's birthday in Chautauqua was to be reminded of the kind of country that I want to raise my children in, and to take part in the kind of conversation I want them to seek out, all their lives, wherever they are. Chautauqua is a performance, but it is also a rehearsal. What skills we learn on this small stage we take home with us for the winter, practice for our role as citizens, and this summer more than ever, we welcomed the chance to build stronger muscles, in anticipation of greater need.

— **Nancy Gibbs**, Editor-at-Large, *Time*

In my boyhood, the Fourth of July was a day set aside for noise. It was, I thought, such a suitable idea that no one I knew could be thanked for it. The Fourth was for small towns as well as for small boys. Things went bang at odd moments all day, but during the late afternoon people would gather in the local park for a potluck picnic. Tables would be covered with white paper but the bandstand would be decked out in red-and-blue bunting. There the town band would play robustly sentimental and patriotic tunes, badly but with beery energy, and a politician or two would speechify, making sounds as meaningless as the caps that went off for no reason other than exuberance. There would be a softball game, sack races, and on the meditative side of the picnic grounds, horseshoes tossed to collar a problem as if they were weighty thoughts. Their clang always seemed calm and immensely reassuring to me, and the men who tossed them at least serious if not wise. They offered, before and after every turn, thoughts, briefly put, on the state of crops, morals and the nation.

The women cleaned after the men had eaten their hamburger, beans and potato salad, then sat about the tables gossiping, fanning away warmth and flies. I saw nothing the matter with any of this . . . I was busy being a boy, and I saw nothing the matter with that either. I threw cherry bombs into the pond where there had been ducks that morning. Too excited to eat sensibly, I rushed from one activity to another, a large red firecracker in my left fist, as real as if it had been drawn by Norman Rockwell, a glorious burst that I was saving for the day's end, which I knew would otherwise be marked by girls waving sparklers and shrieking with glee as they ran to make tracers among the trees.

Sports, food, speeches, music, noise: each a gift of the day that marked our independence, the day that was supposed to repuff our pride and reaffirm our loyalties. My father was an athlete, but he had duties beyond the field of play. He was a veteran of the First World War and a member of the American Legion, so on the morning of the Fourth he would dress himself in puttees, a Sam Browne belt, and a shiny tin helmet; then oil the valves on his cornet, which would have stuck since last fingered, and make a few soft-mouthed toots to hear if his lips were still strong enough to do it. The Legion's small band would turn out for deaths and patriotic anniversaries, either to sound taps or tire out a few Sousa tunes. Then, as the sun set, it would conclude its part in the ceremonies by marching briskly behind the strains of "It's a Grand Old Flag" till both band and flag left the park and were out of sight.

I was in awe of my father's uniform, especially the shiny tin hat I was allowed to fondle, as much as I was of the photographs that showed him in his professional baseball stripes. They were memories for him, symbols for me, full of mystery, for he had been in the world I never knew and fought his war in advance of mine—an improbability that only became reasonable when I pushed my way out of my own past, fleeing my memories as if I had already been in battle a few times before I got decked out as an ensign by Saks Fifth Avenue and wore my one and only tailormades on leave, hoping to appear a person of accomplishment.

The Fourth was more military and more masculine than Memorial Day. Memorial Day was for moms and old men, but on the Fourth we rattled our ceremonial sabres and shot off our toy guns and proclaimed our might and main, resolving to resolve. I eventually learned that such festivities rarely meant a great deal. The holiday was as much about our nation's independence as Christmas was about Christ. At such times we were to spend money and have a good time.

The first Fourth following Pearl Harbor I remember as too serious to be noisy. The Japanese had attacked our fleet as it lay asleep on a sunny Sunday before church. By the time Independence Day arrived we were at war in the full sense, already making many sacrifices, mobilizing our forces, our resources, and suffering humiliating losses every day. I remember being as shocked when Singapore fell as I was about Pearl Harbor. The families of the sailors who died received the thanks of a grateful nation, but these sons had been sailors, after all, not civilians, and had signed a contract that endangered them. Still, when we were drafted we were insured for $10,000 apiece—a policy that I haven't permitted to be cashed yet.

People stayed on their porches that Fourth. There were gas-and-rubber rules that warned folks from the roads, trains were preoccupied by soldiers and their freight, and no one gave a thought to planes. Kids were sent to summer camps, though, because so many moms wanted to visit their husbands while the army bases could be reached. Miniature golf got popular again, and Manhattanites sailed round their island on slow boats or bicycled in packs through startled parks. You had to put a lid on fireworks along the coast because who knew when a bomb burst might be real and the beginning of a German or a Jap attack. Of course we held parades and waved flags. The war had broken the Depression's drought. There were quarters, not pennies, in our pockets. And more of them stayed in those pockets because there was less to be bought. The war forced

Sears, Roebuck to drop antifreeze and accordions from its catalogue, along with alarm clocks and wheelbarrows. They were even out of sheets and pillowcases. Books were a popular item, though soon restrictions on paper would lessen their life span. In most cities the best-seller was Wendell Willkie's *One World* with 1,176,000 copies purchased, except in St. Louis where *The Joy of Cooking,* by the city's own Irma Rombauer, led the list and would eventually circle *One World*'s sales several times.

The Japanese had blown up warships at a naval base because warships were what you fought a war with and they didn't want us to have ours, but the pilots who were flying their first passenger planes that other dreadful morning had symbols as their targets and were borne aloft by the names UNITED and AMERICAN toward twin towers that stood for WORLD-TRADE on a day that would be written "911" in unintended irony. They may have hoped, but they could not have counted on, a photographic coverage so vivid and complete it would bring dismay to a nation and joy to their cause in almost identical moments, and maybe in matching amounts.

The more dismay was ours, the more joy was theirs, for hate has an insatiable appetite and will eat whatever's offered it. Though thousands died, casualties were not the purpose of the attack. There were no islands to be won or lost, no towns to be taken. The World Trade Center had been wounded before; this time they killed it. And the towers fell of their own released weight so that the head was the destroyer of the feet. No Pearl Harbor here. The target was what they believed we stood for: money—money and its power; greed—greed and what it served; arrogance—the arrogance of the rich.

The Terrorists, as we decided to call them, did not smile wryly at the money of the wealthy men who funded them, or at the scams, the lies, the treacheries, the drug sales and robberies that were committed to support their cause. Nor did they examine their own ills, except to blame us for them. They are, and were, the least independent of all men. In exchange for our burning towers, they sent us images of boys throwing rocks and men firing guns at God. They became the bombs that blew up at their festivals. Such shells burst into the only stars their celebrations make: bloody wall spatter and street stain.

Now we have guards at every significant gathering. They peer suspiciously in purses, in bags, at packages that are usually recent purchases, the sales of shoes, at IDs where the poorest possible pictures of ourselves tell them—these strangers—of our harmless hearts, our benevolent selves. At this huge joke no one is allowed to laugh. What bridge, dam, public building, bank, arena, school? What plane, bus, purification plant or power station will be picked on next? Yet terrorists did not set the West on fire. We did. In St. Louis, where I live, thousands gathered at the Arch to listen to western tunes or rock schlock in the early evening, and subsequently to ooh and aah at the fireworks as they have done in the past, though this year there were plastic orange fences everywhere, police busy being noticeable, park rangers searching sacks, National Guardsmen who would have looked natty in their camouflage suits had we been able to see them, and, as consequence of this protection, far fewer people.

In the weeks after 9/11, the homes that row my street were strewn with flags. They hung from attic windows; they rose up on poles stuck in yards; they fluttered like wash from improvised lines. On this Fourth three small grave-size flags were posted in flower boxes near my house. At the last minute, two more were hung down the block. But decals, once prominent on cars, are soiled, banners that flew from antennas have been shredded to indistinctness, bumper stickers have worn out their welcome. It's only a small sample, I know, but it strikes me that the spirit of the Fourth, this year, was used up by September's end and fell like an early leaf.

Instead of fresh defeats, which weekly headed our news after Pearl Harbor, and which refueled our anger and renewed our resolution, other types of towers have fallen, not cities in Asia or islands off Alaska, but those that many corporate entities and financial markets form, with consequences of a different kind: thousands whose jobs have been lost or are now in doubt, savings looted, pensions dissolved, smug and greedy members of small town gambling clubs who have been left holding their handbags while businesses built of money-lust collapsed from moral decay, as nearby, steeples standing for God's good family enterprises sagged from similar fears: tarnish of reputations, drops in contributions, huge losses in civil suits. The terrorists could not have dreamed of luck like the luck they've had, because, though it sometimes seems so, 9/11 was not the cause of our present consternations, our tepid patriotism, our anxieties about the future, our massive mistrust of

our leaders, or the weakening of our faith in Mammon, the god, as our money ought to say, in whom we bank and trust.

The symbol our enemies chose was an appropriate one, and our failure to own up, even now, to what we often fly our flags for—how we are likely to seek justice mainly through litigation, or how our generosity and concerns tend to exhibit themselves by the size of our monetary contributions—is our defenseless underbelly, our possibly incurable weakness, because the fireworks and the crowds are made of money too; the funnel-cake vendors will complain when our custom declines; we shall celebrate as much in shops as at potlucks; our spirits will rise with the markets; we shall win this war without losses, endangering mostly drones; and crab-voiced codgers like me can sweeten the sour taste in our mouths by eating patriotically packaged cookies, available in sacks from machines, born and baked, they say, in the U.S.A., to be offered to the palate in the shape of Uncle Sam himself, or his hat, or Lady Liberty, the letters USA, and even the Grand Old Flag itself, though I notice, as the cookie commences its crumble, that the flag boasts but nine stars . . . well . . . now six. I wonder which States they stood for.

— **William H. Gass**, author of *Tests of Time* and *Reading Rilke*

The Fourth of July was a picture of summer in its glory this year on Martha's Vineyard, where I live. Daylilies and hydrangea were in full flower, the corn in my garden was considerably more than knee-high. The busy harbors of the island looked as cheerful as a scene by Monet.

The day was also about as hot as it gets here off the coast of Massachusetts, with a temperature in the low 90s by midday. The humidity felt like Panama. But by late afternoon when the parade began, a fine breeze was blowing off the water, and the crowds looked every bit as festive as one wants to think of crowds looking everywhere in the country on our national day-of-days, and especially on this first Fourth of July since September 11.

Though there are three principal towns on the island, our Fourth of July parade takes place always in Edgartown, the procession winding through the lovely old back streets, beneath the shade trees, then along by the harbor, before turning up Main Street for what amounts to the grand finale. As parades

go, it's pretty much a small town affair. Summer visitors usually make up half the crowd or more, and this year was no exception. But to my wife and me, watching from the front lawn of St. Elizabeth's Church on Main Street, the crowd looked bigger and seemed more appreciative than ever. There were more flags, more balloons, more star-spangled hats and shirts of all kinds. Antique Buicks and homemade floats rolled by, as in parades past. But then the island's several fire departments marched into view, and the cheer from the crowd might have been for the New York firefighters themselves. When the band broke into "God Bless America," everyone joined in, singing in a way that I had not heard before and that many of us talked about afterward.

Yet nothing so moved me as the sight of one man, Ted Morgan, who, year after year, leads the veterans marching at the head of the parade.

For months now, working on a book, I've been lost in letters and diaries from the Revolutionary War, the larger part written by the officers and men who fought in the American army. And the more I've read, the more I've learned of what happened in the year 1776 especially, the more I've come to appreciate what a near thing it was, and how decisive was the indomitable spirit of a relative few. "Perseverance and spirit have done wonders in all ages," George Washington wrote with absolute conviction early in the struggle, as if he knew more than he let on.

And here now, at the head of our little parade on a summer evening, marched Ted Morgan, a native islander, Selectman, good neighbor, an old familiar face, and I wondered how many who stood watching and cheering had any idea what he had been through in that other dark time of World War II. Still slim and straight at the age of 80, he stepped along like a man half his age.

Enlisting in the army at 19, soon after Pearl Harbor, Ted Morgan served as a paratrooper in Sicily and Italy. As part of the 82nd Airborne he parachuted into Normandy on D-Day before dawn. He fought in the Battle of the Bulge and on into Germany until the German surrender. There in the dappled light on Main Street in his own hometown, he seemed to me the personification of what we need to remember and honor in the aftermath of September 11, the very essence of the strength that is in us, and I cheered and clapped until my hands ached.

Call it spirit, call it patriotism, grit, call it heart, it is what carried the day during the Revolution and so many trials since, and will again, we may be certain.

— **David McCullough**, author of *John Adams*

Mandan, N.Dak/Steve Simon

Last September the artist, poet, filmmaker and longtime LIFE photographer Gordon Parks was moved to remember the 11th in word and imagery. On the Fourth of July, 2002, he again recorded his thoughts in a poem and a picture.

God, the Devil and September by Gordon Parks

Four planes. A nightmarish morning.
Nineteen madmen who, for incalculable reasons,
shunned peace and embraced hatred.
Now it seems awesomely clear;
universal brotherhood must grow used to our absence.
Suddenly, caught in the grip of the enemy's teeth,
our skyscape had shuddered, then like a fantasy,
burst into the beauteous glow of a terrorist's dream.
What we learned on that terrible morning
is, by far, too much to rub off the blackboard.
The mothering earth is smouldering,

cracking and ruthlessly tearing apart.
The enemy still threatens our lives,
and we ask leave to destroy him
in order that our children might live.

Perhaps that would be next to nothing.
Then it could be very close to everything.
But just how long can humanity put up with dying?

Never have I seen so many flags
on windows, doors, cars and lapels.
Rippling in the wind they speak proudly
about lives that were saved,
    and harshly
about deaths that littered the sky.
No, they leave nothing untouched—
on buildings, on clothing, on cars.
And surely they wave with pride,
    and with good reason.
They rose above the fire and smoke
and refused to be entombed in fear.

Near ten months have passed.
Yet that horrible Tuesday refuses to age.
The absence of those who perished that day
will forever feed the memory of those
    who were left behind.

Despite our appointment with tragedy
July Fourth still grasps its place in eternity.
But it would be an exotic moment
if, on that day of our Independence,
the entire universe would come together
to speak a beautiful language called love.
Wars of bombs and gas amount to victories
    without victors.
Even a survivor would be lost
in the cold ashes of a dead city.

Today, Liberty by Eddie Adams

1968

This was to be the greatest photograph I ever made. I was lying flat on the shaking ground, as flat as I could make myself. It was 1968 during the Vietnam War. I was with a company of Marines pinned down on a hill under heavy enemy fire from rockets, mortars, grenades. Hugging the ground four or five feet from me was a handsome U.S. Marine. The boy was a cliché: light brown hair, blue eyes, square jaw, pale skin burned by the sun, about 18 years old. But in his glassy eyes I could see fear. Fear had frozen his expression, stamped it with the realization and horror that war was real, war was loud, war was shaking the earth he lay on. I slid my camera in front of me, framed his face and positioned myself to squeeze the shutter. I hesitated. A grenade exploded, sending a spray of dirt over us both. Again I moved the camera to my eye, hesitated, and couldn't push the button. I made a third, feeble attempt . . . never capturing his face on film.

2001

Thirty-three years later, on September 11, two airplanes struck buildings only a few minutes from where I live. My young son was a witness to the event. After verifying his safety, I began to prepare my cameras and load film while watching live coverage on TV. The more I watched the more my heart began to bleed. The biggest story in the world was unfolding in my backyard, and I kept telling myself, *What are you waiting for? Just go!* I made several attempts towards the front door. For the second time in my life I hesitated, gripped with a kind of paralysis, moving between fascination, horror and disbelief. In the end, I did not go. This was not about my own safety. Once again, I realized, it had become too personal.

2002

Out on assignment to cover the Fourth, I am still feeling numb, wondering if not enough time has gone by to absorb the effects of that terrible day on me, my family, all of America. I am trying to think of a way to make a picture that will absolve all that has passed and make me feel better. Maybe it will be a closeup of an innocent child, an older couple, a weathered World War II veteran at a parade, an immigrant family, my son who saw the towers (but this time free, at play). The possibilities seem endless in a land of liberty. Liberty. Maybe it will be Liberty.

TRIBUTE: New York

In the year since September 11,
memorials have risen from sea
to shining sea. In late winter, beams
of light shot heavenward from
where the first blow had been struck.
Photograph by Melvin Levine

For 32 nights beginning on the six-month anniversary of the attacks, "Tribute in Light," composed of two parallel beams formed by 88 searchlights, projected a mile into the sky. Organizer Saskia Levy likened the lights to "a votive candle."

TRIBUTE: North Carolina

Working with massive steel beams from the World Trade Center site, a sculptor creates art from "battle-scarred relics" and inspires hope where once there was only sorrow and death. Photography by Abigail Seymour

In Manhattan they threw lights into the sky, while the schoolkids of Scottsdale, Ariz., built a 1,500-pound flag out of mosaic tiles. Everyone wanted—needed—to do something. In Greensboro, N.C., sculptor Jim Gallucci found himself "numbed by the whole thing. All I wanted was to go home and hug my wife and children. Then I asked what all of America was asking: 'How can I help?' I thought: 'Do what you do. Make art.'" Gallucci got approval from a firm involved in the WTC recovery effort, then went to a scrap yard in New Jersey where "they said, 'Take all you want.' I picked out five pieces of steel that I felt had significance." The 16 tons of beams were carted to Greensboro, and Gallucci and 10 assistants set to work.

Gallucci's recent sculptures have included many gates and doorways; the current project is called "Gates of Sorrow." He says, "Gates symbolize passage—a physical, emotional and spiritual movement from one space or consciousness to another. Individually and collectively, September 11 was an important passage for mankind."

In the workshop, Gallucci welds, Catherine Cravens drafts, and others come and go, donating time. Their collective efforts will, in the end, yield a 50-ton, 47-foot-high sculpture that will tour the country. Says Gallucci of the project: "It's been a real spiritual ride."

A WORLD ALTERED

On December 7, 1941, a surprise attack "awakened a sleeping giant." Six decades later, America was again violently awakened.

Mario Tama/Getty

Steve Liss/Gamma

Shortly after Americans learned of the valor displayed on September 11, old-fashioned heroes became fresh once more. At far left, three-year-old Samuel Liberman proudly shows off his Halloween firefighter outfit in New York City. Above: This is no holiday for the Cicero family of Chicago, who are trying on gas masks in deadly earnest. Fear of bioterrorism spread rapidly.

Ezra Shaw/Allsport/Getty

Going places has become a lot more complicated, and many sectors of the economy have suffered in the new climate. The woman at left is being frisked by a security guard before a football game at Foxboro Stadium in Massachusetts. Many of the formerly familiar accoutrements at a game, like coolers, are often taboo. Above, on Christmas Eve, a man and his shoes are scrutinized at Eastern Iowa Airport in Cedar Rapids. Long lines and airport evacuations have made air travel a nettlesome chore, but most people keep their grumbling to a minimum. Opposite: precautionary measures in New York City.

Nina Berman/Aurora

In the heart of New York City's Rockefeller Center (above), people grow uneasy as a news ticker reveals on October 12 that an employee of NBC—whose building is a stone's throw away—has tested positive for anthrax. The spores were transmitted by mail. Below, a letter carrier in Santa Monica resorts to latex gloves and a surgical mask. Right: Hazardous material workers emerge from an anthrax search of the Dirksen Senate Office Building in Washington, D.C.

Stefano Paltera/Gamma

Alex Wong/Getty

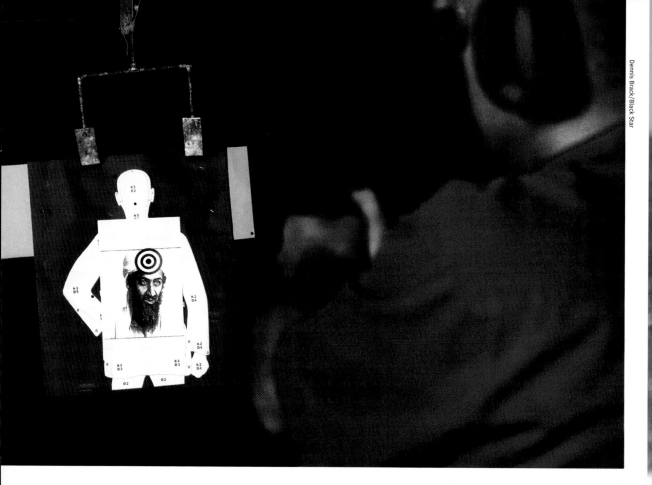

Dennis Brack/Black Star

Above, in Chantilly, Va., not far from the headquarters of the NRA, Osama bin Laden is an oft-requested target at the Blue Ridge shooting range. Military personnel became ubiquitous at airports and train stations, with "high alerts" issued with disturbing frequency. Their armed presence is comforting if also chilling. Below, Air National Guard Maj. Ted Kobierski works New York's Grand Central Terminal.

Mario Tama/Getty

Andrea Booher/FEMA

The variety of precautions now taken in America are all too sundry. For example, security has always been taut for an Olympics, but at the 2002 Salt Lake City Winter Games, entirely new measures were called for. Above, in nearby Big Cottonwood Canyon, ski patroller Keith Sternfels and nine-month-old black Labrador–Border collie Chaco prepare for terrorist-wrought avalanches.

BELATED CONDOLENCES

In a faraway corner of Kenya, word of the September 11 attacks was slow in coming but touched the heart of a village. Photography by Mariella Furrer

The Masai of East Africa are renowned for their courage and skill as warriors. To be all that they can be, young males between the ages of 14 and 30, known as *morans,* live alone in the bush, developing the wisdom and endurance that mark the tribe. Kimeli Naiyomah, however, has taken a different path. He is a premed student at Stanford who will return to his village after he gets his M.D. On September 11, Naiyomah was visiting New York and saw the horrors firsthand. In May he went back to Kenya for a ceremony. Some in his village had heard vague stories about a disaster but all were stunned by what he told them. "They couldn't believe that people could jump from a building so high that they would die when they reached the ground," said Naiyomah. Thereafter, unpopular villagers were referred to as Osamas. "We don't have anyone as cruel as him," said 44-year-old James Ngodia. "If he comes to Masailand, we will surely kill him with our spears and arrows." That event, however, is for the future. The Masai wanted to do something right away. Cows are of incomparable value to them, "almost the center of life for us," said Naiyomah. Fourteen cows were donated by the villagers to America to express the Masai's sorrow, and their thanks for taking care of Naiyomah. Said Ngodia, "When America is hurting, we want to share their pain."

The blessing of the cows features ornate garb and solemn song. At top right, U.S. envoy William Brencick is greeted by tribal chiefs. Brencick said that because of shipping difficulties, the cows would be sold and the profits used to buy Masai beadwork that would be sent to America.

LIFE

UNITED WE STAND

JULY 6, 1942 **10** CENTS
YEARLY SUBSCRIPTION $4.50

REG. U. S. PAT. OFF.

In a "patriotic conspiracy," hundreds of magazines put Old Glory on their covers in the summer of '42. That campaign, which rallied support for the war effort, is being recalled in an exhibition at the Smithsonian's National Museum of American History in Washington, D.C. In 2002 the flags serve the same purpose they did 60 years ago.